SOVIETICA

PUBLICATIONS OF THE INSTITUTE OF EAST-EUROPEAN STUDIES

UNIVERSITY OF FRIBOURG/SWITZERLAND

Edited by

J. M. BOCHENSKI

SHORT HANDBOOK OF COMMUNIST

IDEOLOGY

SHORT HANDBOOK

OF COMMUNIST

IDEOLOGY

Synopsis of the 'Osnovy marksizma-leninizma'

with complete index

Selected by

HELMUT FLEISCHER

D. REIDEL PUBLISHING COMPANY / DORDRECHT-HOLLAND

Kleines Textbuch der kommunistischen Ideologie

Published by D. Reidel Publishing Company / Dordrecht-Holland

Translated from the German in concordance with the Russian by T. J. Blakeley

Printed in The Netherlands by D. Reidel, Dordrecht

FOREWORD

We have once again decided to publish in our series a source-text for the study of Communist ideology. This synopsis of *Principles of Marxism-Leninism* [1] (published at the end of 1959 and widely distributed in the Soviet Union) appears as a sequel to that of the *Principles of Marxist Philosphy* which I published in 1959 as *The Dogmatic Principles of Soviet Philosphy*. This book is a corporate work, done by some forty Soviet philosophers, sociologists, economists, Party-theoreticians and propagandists, under the direction of O. V. Kuusinen (member of the Praesidium of the Communist Party of the Soviet Union).

Except for a few clarifications, we have restricted ourselves to presenting the most important parts of the original text in an original translation which provides the material, in an authentic and handy [2] form, for our Institute's courses in Sovietology. In comparison to the other parts, the philosophical portions (Sections 1 and 2) have been held to a minimum since they repeat, for the most part, material which is already available in the synopsis of the *Principles of Marxist Philosophy*.

I wish to thank the Rockefeller Foundation for their support which has made possible the research of our Institute as well as the preparation of the present work.

J. M. BOCHEŃSKI

[1] The original Russian title is: *Osnovy marksizma-leninizma*. Učebnoe posobie (Textbook), Gosudarstvennoe izdatel'stvo političeskoj literatury (State Publishing House for Political Literature), Moskva, 1959, 774 pages, 300 000 copies.
[2] The official German translation (Dietz, Berlin, 1960) with 840 pages and the English (Moscow, 1963) with 735 pages are anything but handy.

V

INTRODUCTION

No other political-social movement in world history has had an action-program based on such comprehensive and extensive theoretical considerations comparable to that of contemporary Communism. After many expansions and revisions, the beginnings made by Karl Marx and Friedrich Engels – often admittedly fragmentary – have given rise to the almost universal doctrinal structure of contemporary, post-Stalinist Marxism-Leninism, which has already fascinated many of our contemporaries by its fullness and completeness, and which definitely represents a world-wide intellectual force of the highest significance.

Recently there has been a significant progress in the systematic presentation of this doctrine. Since 1956 there has appeared a constantly growing number of basic texts and encyclopedias for the various domains of specialization.[1]

Among these texts and encyclopedic presentations – which, of course, are accompanied by extensive specialized works and articles – the *Principles of Marxism-Leninism* has a special place. It is not really a 'summa' of the Marxist-Leninist world-view. As the authors themselves say, this would hardly be possible in one book. But, it does present the doctrine in a systematic form not hitherto available, i.e. the general, philosophic understanding of the world (First Section), the interpretation of human society and of its historical process (Second Section), the diagnostic of and prognostic for bourgeois society (Third Section), the strategic outlook for war against this social order (Fourth Section) and, finally, the directives for the construction of the new world-order, an essential element of which is already completed in the Soviet Union so

---

[1] Here are some of the more important titles: *Great Soviet Encyclopedia* (53 vols.), *Small Soviet Encyclopedia* (10 vols.), *Soviet Historical Encyclopedia* (12 vols.), *Literary Encyclopedia* (6 vols.), *Philosophical Encyclopedia* (4 vols.), *Theatrical Encyclopedia* (4 vols.), *Pedagogical Encyclopedia* (3 vols.), *Youth-Encyclopedia* (10 vols.), *Film Lexicon* (2 vols.), *World History* (10 vols.), *History of the U.S.S.R.*, *History of the C.P.S.U.*, over a dozen compendia of the philosophic principles of diamat or diahistomat, principles of epistemology, logical compendia, textbooks of Communist morality, of Marxist-Leninist ethics and of Communist education, many texts on scientific atheism, esthetics, political economy, the political economy of socialism, the bases of political theory, history of philosophy (6 vols. and 1 vol.), history of political and social doctrines.

that the doctrine on socialism and Communism is not only a project but also a theoretical interpretation of Soviet society (Fifth Section). This selection constitutes something like a 'big catechism' where every Party member (and, in addition, every active citizen of socialist society) finds what he needs. Its factual statements (Sections 3 to 5) form a sort of explicit commentary to the new program of the CPSU. The real novelty is the systematic presentation of Communist 'political ideology' in the more restricted sense of the term (Sections 4 and 5), which hitherto was included in the history of the Party or in historical materialism. These sections, which are to be taken literally as a 'guide to action', are given a more thorough treatment than the other, more theoretical, sections (economy is only partially treated). For reasons stated in the Foreword, we have turned our selection even more in favor of these practical themes, as the following breakdown shows:

	Number of Pages	
	Original	Synopsis
1. Philosophic principles (diamat)	105	6
2. Materialist conception of history	98	11
3. Capitalist economy	84	13
4. Theory of the Communist movement	215	22
5. Socialism and Communism	219	39

Our intention is to show, on the basis of the Soviet texts themselves, how N. S. Khrushchov's partisans currently interpret the world-system and its developmental tendencies. We have not discussed their theses since only a superficial commentary could be made of such an abbreviated presentation, and since we did not wish to emulate those Soviet publishers of Western texts who make great use of prefaces, postscripts and notes to destroy that with which they disagree. This book is primarily intended for students who have a particular Sovietological interest in their main field of study – e.g. in Soviet philosophy, historiography, physics, education, etc. – and who want an over-all view of Soviet ideology. In the course of their studies, they themselves will locate the areas where there are special problems and which need further development, and themes on which critical comment is necessary. However, genuine criticism can only be made on the basis of the specialized literature. Only in this way, and gradually, will we contribute to elevating the ideological East-West conflict from the Agitprop sphere to a higher, scientific, level.

To facilitate classroom use, we have serially numbered the selections in the margin. At the end of each selection the parentheses contain the page reference to the Russian original.

HELMUT FLEISCHER

Translator's note: The German word *Gesetzmäßigkeit* (for the Russian *zakonomernost'*) has, at least in certain contexts, no exact equivalent in English. It designates that order, regularity, or uniformity which is the basis of a law. Thus, the 'Law of Gravity' is based on the observation of a certain order or regularity in physical events, e.g. in the fall of objects or parabolic flight of projectiles. Therefore, we have variously translated *Gesetzmäßigkeit* as 'order', 'regularity' or 'uniformity', as the context and sentence structure demanded. In the case of the cognate adjective, *gesetzmäßig*, we have in some places used 'law-bound'.

Weltanschauung (for *mirovozzrenie*) has everywhere been given as 'world-outlook' or 'world-view' even though this does not carry all the force of the German word.

TABLE OF CONTENTS

TABLE OF CONTENTS

NAMES OF THE AUTHORS OF THE BOOK

"The book was written by a group of scholars, Party-workers and propagandists. The main work was done by: O. V. Kuusinen (Director), Ju. A. Arbatov, A. S. Beljakov, S. L. Vygodskij, A. A. Makarovskij, A. G. Milejkovskij, E. P. Sitkovskij and L. M. Šejdin.

Collaborators on single chapters: K. N. Brutenc, F. M. Burlackij, N. I. Ivanov, I. S. Kon, B. M. Lejbzon, N. V. Matkovskij, Ju. K. Mel'vil', D. E. Mel'nikov, L. A. Mendel'son, C. A. Stepanjan, S. G. Strumilin. Further, some questions were elaborated on the basis of materials provided by: V. F. Asmus, A. N. Kuznecov, B. P. Kuznecov, Ju. N. Semenov, I. S. Smirnov, and P. S. Čeremnyx.

Valuable advice and hints were provided by: for philosophy – Corresponding Member of the AN SSSR[1] A. D. Aleksandrov, Corr. Memb. B. M. Vul, Prof. G. M. Gak, Prof. G. E. Glezerman, Corr. Memb. F. V. Konstantinov, Corr. Memb. X. S. Koštojanc, Prof. M. M. Rozental', Corr. Memb. P. N. Fedoseev; for history of science – Member of the AN SSSR A. N. Nesmejanov; for economy – Corr. Memb. A. A. Arzumanjan, Acad. Memb. E. S. Varga, Prof. L. M. Gatovskij, Corr. Memb. L. A. Leont'ev; for Chapter 25 – Corr. Memb. Ju. P. Francev. Useful indications came from other responsible Party and government authorities."

(From the Foreword, p. 4)

---

[1] *Akademija nauk* = Academy of Sciences of the U.S.S.R.

THE PHILOSOPHIC PRINCIPLES OF
THE MARXIST-LENINIST WORLD-VIEW

Chapter 1

PHILOSOPHIC MATERIALISM

The unshakeable foundation of the whole Marxist-Leninist doctrinal 1
structure is its philosophic doctrine, dialectical and historical materialism.
This philosophic doctrine takes the world as it is and carries out its investi-
gations in accord with the results of progressive science and social
practice. Marxist philosophic materialism is the law-bound result of the
century-long development of scientific knowledge. (13)

Materialist philosophy begins with the recognition of the fact that nature 2
(stars; sun; the earth with its mountains and plains, seas and woods;
beasts and men who are gifted with consciousness and the power to think)
exists. Supernatural phenomena or forces do not and cannot exist. (15)

The question of the relationship of human consciousness to material 3
being is the basic question of every philosophy... Which is basic –
nature or thought? According to the answer given this question, philosophers are divided into two large camps. Those who accept a material
principle, nature, as fundamental and consider thought or spirit as a
property of matter belong to the camp of *materialism*. On the other
hand, those who maintain that thought, spirit, or the idea existed prior
to nature, that nature has – in one way or another – been made by and is
dependent on a spiritual principle form the camp of idealism. (15)

In Marxist philosophical materialism the concept 'matter' is used in its 4
widest sense – to indicate all that which objectively, i.e. independent of
consciousness, exists and is reflected in human perceptions. (22) Matter is
the philosophic concept for the designation of the objective world. The
physical structure of the world and its physical properties are the object
of physics. (23) Matter is uncreatable and indestructible. It changes
constantly but not even one of its particles can cease to exist. (23)

Motion (change, development) is the eternal and inalienable property of 5
matter.... The multiformity of matter bespeaks the multiformity of the

1

forms of its motion. The simplest form of the motion of matter is the mechanical change of place of a body in space. A more complex form of motion is to be found (for example) in thermal processes and the un-ordered motion of the molecules which make up physical bodies. Science has established that light, electro-magnetic rays and physical fields are also specific forms of self-moving matter. The motion of matter also comes to light in the chemical processes of change of state ... Life in organic nature, the physiological processes in plants and animals, the development of the species – all these are also specific forms of motion, the universal property of matter. We see an especially complex form of the motion of matter in the social life of man, i.e. the development of material production, commercial life, etc. (25).

6   The ability to think – which is proper to man – is the product of a lengthy development of the organic world. (29) Consciousness is the product of the activity of the human brain which is bound up with a complex of sense-organs. Essentially, it is a reflection of the material world. (32)

7   The greatest historical contribution of materialist philosophy is the fact that it helps man to free himself from superstition. Even in antiquity it had come out against the fear of death, of the gods and of other super-natural forces. Materialist philosophy teaches man not to hope in the other life but to value earthly life and to strive for its amelioration. (18)

Chapter 2

THE MATERIALIST DIALECTIC

8   The materialist dialectic is the most profound, universal and contentful doctrine on motion and development.... The founders of Marxism ... understood the dialectic as the doctrine on the universal relations and most general developmental laws of all of reality. (54–55)

9   The most universal relation – known to every man and met by him always and everywhere – is that between cause and effect (i.e. 'causal' ...). (58) Recognition of the strict causal determination of all phenomena is, at the same time, recognition of necessity's reign in the world. (61) Laws are the most perfect expression of necessity in nature and society ... The law is a deeper, more essential, more constant, and always repeated

relation or dependence between phenomena or the different sides of one and the same phenomenon. (62) Among the multifarious phenomena of nature and human society there are also those which do not come to be with necessity out of the law-bound development of the matter concerned or of a given series of events ... but which could not come to be or come to be in another way. These are accidental phenomena. (63)

QUANTITATIVE AND QUALITATIVE CHANGES

The totality of the essential traits or characteristics which distinguish any given thing, is called the *quality* of the thing or phenomenon. (67) It is only the concept of those distinctive traits which cannot be thought away, of the internal structure of the phenomenon which constitutes its being determined and without which it ceases to exist as such ... In addition to quality, each thing also has a quantitative side, is marked by specific *quantitative* indices on which its quality comes to be. (68)   10

Quantitative changes are more or less gradual and are often hardly noticeable. At first they do not essentially affect the qualitative state of the thing, but in the further accumulation and final analysis they lead to a basic, qualitative change of the thing. One says, 'quantity changes to quality' ... The dialectical transition of quantity to quality is particularly important for the understanding of the processes of development since it explains the coming to be of a new quality without which there is no development. ... The transition of quantitative changes to basic, qualitative changes and vice versa is a universal *developmental law of the dialectic*. It appears in all processes of nature, society and thought – wherever the old is replaced by the new. (71).   11

The transition of a thing from one qualitative state to another, new, state as a result of the accumulation of quantitative changes is a *leap* in development. The leap is an interruption in the gradual quantitative changes of the thing; it forms a transition to a new quality; it means a sudden switch, a basic change in development. (71–72)   12

OPPOSITIONS AS SOURCE OF DEVELOPMENT

Now arises the question: what is the motive force and origin of all development? The answering of this question is one of the most important   13 tasks of the dialectic. In answering it, the point of departure is the contradictory character of the whole of reality. (74) Hegel called the coexistence of opposed aspects in one phenomenon a 'contradiction'... The founders of Marxism, who materialistically reworked the Hegelian dialectic, conserved the expression 'contradiction' but gave it another, materialistic sense. Under dialectical contradiction Marxism understands the presence of opposite and mutually exclusive aspects in one phenomenon or in one process; aspects which, however, presuppose each other and which – within the phenomenon in question – can exist only in a reciprocal relationship. (75–76) As a matter of fact, one discovers in the study of any phenomena in nature, in social relations, or in the spiritual life of man, contradictions, i.e. the collision of opposed aspects or tendencies. (76)

14   In nature, social life and man's thought, development takes place in such a way that opposed and mutually exclusive aspects or tendencies come to light in an object; they enter into "battle" which leads to the annihilation of the old and to the appearance of new forms... This is the law of development. "Development is a 'battle' of opposites", wrote V. I. Lenin. (77).

15   In reference to social life it is important to distinguish between antagonistic and non-antagonistic contradictions. *Antagonistic* contradictions are those between social groups or classes whose basic interests are irreconcilable... Antagonistic contradictions are historically conditioned; they are generated by class-society and persist as long as this type of society lasts. *Non-antagonistic* contradictions... are those of a society where the basic interests of the classes, the social groups, coincide. Therefore, the solution of such contradictions comes not through class-war but through the common efforts of the friendly classes. (79–80)

DEVELOPMENT FROM THE LOWER TO THE HIGHER

16   The continuous appearance of ever newer forms and the inevitable dissolution of old forms through the new gives evidence of the eternal motion and development of matter... Hegel called the dissolution of one form of being by another 'negation'... Marx and Engels conserved the term 'negation' and materialistically interpreted it... In the Marxist

4

dialectic negation is understood as the dissolution – occurring ordinarily in the process of development – of the old quality by a new one which issues from the old one. (83) Dialectical 'negation' does not presuppose the mere annihilation of the old but also the preservation of the more viable elements of earlier stages of development ...

To the extent that in the process of development only that is 'negated' 17 which has become old and all that is healthy and viable is preserved, development is movement forward, a rise from lower to higher, from simple to complex, i.e. progress. Often there appears in the course of this development something like a return to earlier stages when there is repetition in the new forms of certain characteristics of already passed and dissolved forms. Thus, the primitive tribal society in which there was no exploitation was dissolved in the course of history by exploiter-society. With the transition to socialism the exploitation of man by man will be eliminated ... (84–86)

The process of development can be marked by deviations from the 18 progressive line; there are zig-zags, reverses, periods of extended immobility. However, as history shows, the forward motion prevails in the end over all these temporary deviations and impediments and imposes itself... Since the materialist dialectic traces this progressive development of nature, society, and human thought, it arms man with a scientifically established optimism and helps him in the fight for new and higher forms of life and social organization. (86)

Chapter 3

EPISTEMOLOGY

The Marxist theory of knowledge is the *reflection theory*. This means that 19 it considers knowledge to be the mirroring of objective reality in the human brain. (96) If our perceptions, representations, concepts and theories correspond to objective reality and correctly reflect it, then we say they are true. (99) At any given moment, the knowledge acquired by science is marked by a certain incompleteness and imperfection ... The incompleteness and imperfection of human knowledge ... is usually termed the relativity of human knowledge ... In our constantly relative knowledge there is an objectively true content which is preserved in the process of knowledge and which serves as basis for the further development of knowledge. This permanent content of relative truths in human knowledge is designated as the true content or simply as absolute truth. (105–106)

20 Unlike previous materialism, Marxism includes practice in epistemology, considering it to be the basis and goal of the knowing process and also as criterion for the admissibility of knowledge. (93)

THE MATERIALIST CONCEPTION OF HISTORY

Chapter 4

THE ESSENCE OF HISTORICAL MATERIALISM

The revolution which Marx and Engels carried out in the social sciences   **21** consists above all in the fact that they showed the non-existence of any mysterious, supernatural force in society, and showed that man himself is the creator of history... On the other hand, Marxism established that men do not arbitrarily create their history but do so on the basis of the objective, material conditions left to them by previous generations. Thereby voluntarism and subjectivism are eliminated and the way to the understanding of history as a law-bound process is open. (120)

MEANS OF PRODUCTION AS THE MATERIAL FOUNDATION OF THE LIFE OF SOCIETY

Marx formulated the original thesis of historical materialism as follows: **22** "It is not the consciousness of men which determines their being but, vice versa, their social being which determines their consciousness"... He is speaking, of course, not of the being and consciousness of single men but of larger groups (classes, social levels, and, ultimately, all of society), i.e. not of individual being and consciousness but of social being and social consciousness... Social being is the material life of society in all its complexity and contradictions. (120–121)

The material life of society is, above all, the productive activity of men,   **23** which is directed toward the production of things and goods which are vital necessities (food, clothing, shelter, etc.)... As Engels says, men must first eat, drink, be clothed and have shelter before they can busy themselves with politics, science, art, religion, etc. (121) Instruments of production, with which material goods are made, and men, who carry out production on the basis of previous experience, form the *forces of production* of society. (122) Marx and Engels called *relations of production* those relations which men enter into in the course of the production of material goods. They are also called commercial and property relations since their character depends on who owns the means of production...

Historical materialism uses the expression *means of production* to indicate the unity of forces of production and relations of production. (123) In a class-society, once these relations have come into existence, they are institutionalized politically and juridically in the forms of ownership, in laws, in class-politics, in the state, etc. (125)

24 The unity of the forces of production and of the relations of production ... in no way excludes contradictions between them ... With the growth of the forces of production, there necessarily arises between them and the relations of production a lack of agreement which, in the end, leads to conflict since the superannuated relations of production impede the growth of the forces of production. (125) The conflict between relations of production and forces of production leads to the increase of contradictions in various domains of social life and, in the first place, between the classes, some of which have identified their interests with the old property relations and others with the new ones. (125)

BASE AND SUPERSTRUCTURE

25 The dominant form of ownership determines the social stratification of society, i.e. its class-composition which, in turn, determines the character of the political institutions and the juridical norms. (126) The same must be said of philosophic, religious, moral, artistic and other social ideas and representations. (127) The state of the forces of production ... determines the character of human relations of production, i.e. the economic structure of society. In turn, this economic structure is the *base* (foundation) on which the multiple social relations, ideas and institutions are built. The social ideas (political, juridical, philosophical, religious, etc.), the institutions and organizations (state, church, political parties, etc.) which come to be on a given base form the *superstructure* of society. . . . Every society is an organic unity, a so-called *social-economic formation,* i.e. a definite historical type of society with means of production, base and superstructure which are specific to it. (126, 128)

HISTORY AS THE DEVELOPMENT AND DISSOLUTION OF SOCIAL-ECONOMIC FORMATIONS

26 Scientifically admissible knowledge of the past permits us to say that the history of mankind is a series of social-economic formations. There have

8

been a total of four: primitive, slave-holding, feudal and capitalist – and mankind is now in the transition period to the next formation, Communism, the first phase of which is called socialism. (129)

Primitive society. Work-tools were very primitive at this stage.... Only   27
work in common ... of all members of the primitive society, i.e. their solidarity and mutual help, enabled them to produce the necessary means of existence. The production of each was hardly enough to nourish him who produced it. A surplus which could have been used to help other members of society simply did not exist ... Even though primitive society was free from the senselessness and horror which later marked the exploiter-societies, it was by no means the 'golden age' of mankind. (129–130).

Slave-holding society. The basis of the relations of production in this   28
social order is the private ownership by the slave-owner not only of the tools of production but also of those who worked, the slaves.... The slave era brought the worker terrible burdens and sufferings ... The brutal exploitation of the slave lead to bitter revolt. In order to keep him in line, a special apparatus of oppression, the state, had to be invented.

Nonetheless, slave-holding society was an important step forward in the   29
development of mankind ... Massive use of slave-labor made possible the construction of dams, irrigation systems, roads, ships, canals and large cities. And the liberation – thanks to the exploitation of the slaves – of a part of society from direct participation in production set the stage for the development of science and art.... But, the time comes when the growth-possibilities of the slave-holding means of production are exhausted because its relations of production become more and more of a drag on the further development of the forces of production. Finally, slave-holding society falls under the combined weight of revolts by the workers and attacks by the neighboring barbarian tribes.... A new formation, feudalism, comes to be. (131–133)

Feudalism. The basis of the relations of production of this social order is   30
the ownership by the feudal lords of the means of production, mainly the earth.... The serfs were dependent on the lord but did not completely belong to him.... In feudal society the peasants and artisans also had personal property.... This particularity in the relations of production

9

opened new possibilities for the growth of the forces of production. The direct producer developed a certain material interest in the result of his work.... Though the forms of exploitation were milder than those of slavery, they were still terrible. The exploitation of the peasant was based, as always, on extra-economic force. (133–134)

31   Large-scale manufacturing grew up beside small artisanal enterprises.... Gradually, a new – capitalist – means of production developed within feudal society. Its further development required the liquidation of the feudal order.... Thus began the era of bourgeois revolutions. (135–136)

32   *Capitalism.* Private ownership by the capitalists of the means of production bases the relations of production here. The capitalist class exploits the wage-worker class which is personally free but must sell its work since it owns no means of production.... The relations between them are antagonistic since it is based on the exploitation and domination of the have-nots by the haves.... But the methods of exploitation and domination have changed – economic pressure is the most common.... With change in methods of exploitation, come changes in political domination.... The absolute power of the hereditary monarch is replaced by the parliamentary republic; the right to vote and the freedom and equality of the citizen are proclaimed. (136)

33   Capitalist relations of production open up wide possibilities for the development of the forces of production.... As has been today established not only in theory but also in social practice, capitalism too is temporary and transitional. More and more insoluble antagonisms ripen within it. ... The only escape from these contradictions is the transition to social ownership of the means of production, i.e. to socialism. (136–137)

34   *Socialism.* The socialist means of production are based on social ownership of the tools of production. This is why the relations of production of socialist society are relations of cooperation and mutual help of creators who are free from exploitation.... The new social order opens to mankind unlimited possibilities of progress not only in the domain of the development of the forces of production but also in all other domains of the life of society. (137–138)

HISTORICAL LAWS AND THE CONSCIOUS ACTIVITY OF MEN

The development of society is a law-bound process based on a specific   35
historical necessity which depends neither on man's will nor on his
consciousness.... Nonetheless, the laws according to which society
develops are not automatic. These laws are formed as the result of human
activity and, in turn, determine the general trend of human activity.
Without men and their activities, there can be no social laws ... These
laws determine the course of history only through the doings, conflicts
and strivings of millions of men. (138–139)

Marxism-Leninism – because it regards the social law dialectically –   36
understands that it works in the form of a dominant tendency in the
development of the social relations in question. This means that the law
determines the general line of development, which necessarily follows
from certain objective conditions. But social development is contradictory
and the concrete course of events depends not only on general laws but
also on the factual relation of class-strengths, the policies of the conflicting
classes and many other specific conditions.... The fight of the working
class expresses historical necessity but its success depends in any instant
on many factors.... The effect of one factor can bring the working class
closer to victory, while that of another can only hinder it. But, in the end,
the triumph of the working class and the victory of socialism are unavoidable. (139–140).

Since historical regularity is expressed in the activity of man, the great   37
importance of social ideas is evident. New ideas calling for change of the
social order come to be and are spread when the development of the
material life of society puts man before new tasks. (140–141)

The development of all social formations previous to socialism was such   38
that the objective laws worked with blind necessity finding their way
through the accidental, uncoordinated activities of the individuals. The
objective laws ruled over men and were seen by them as foreign and
uncomprehended forces to which they had to submit.... Private ownership of the means of production does not permit conscious direction of
the development of society.... Divided into inimical classes, society has
no common will which would direct its development in the direction
dictated by objective laws. (143) The social revolution of the proletariat

11

is the first in history in which the revolutionary vanguard of the working masses – the Marxist-Leninist Party – is clearly conscious of the objective meaning of their historic actions. . . . Under socialism men are able to control production throughout society thanks to social ownership of the means of production. (144)

39   Conscious use of social laws by man does not affect their objective character but permits society to freely orient itself in any situation and, having correctly viewed the objective conditions, to proceed by plan to the established goal which has been established on the basis of knowledge of these laws. Man cannot change the law of gravity. . . . Even less can society arbitrarily establish the development-proportion of the major branches of the economy . . . (144)

Chapter 5

CLASSES, CLASS-WAR AND THE STATE

40   The most complete definition of classes was given by V. I. Lenin in "The Great Initiative": "Classes are large human groups which are distinct because of their place in a historically determined system of social production, because of their (to a great extent fixed and formulated in laws) relation to the means of production, because of their role in the social organization of work and, consequently, because of the size of their share of social wealth and their method of obtaining it. Classes are groups of men, such that one can gain possession of the work of the other because of the distinctness of its place in a determined system of social economy." . . . It is not the 'will of God' and not the individual traits of men – as pretend the ideologists of the exploiter-classes – but the belonging to this or that class which explains the dominant, privileged position of one and the oppression, poverty and lack of rights of the other. (155)

Of course, this does not mean that all other differences and relations, other than those of class, are not essential . . .[1]

[1] Besides the archaic forms (tribe, clan, ethnic group) there are the nation and the race. "By nation Marxism-Leninism understands a historically established, stable community of language, territory, economy and physical characteristics as exemplified in community of culture." (according to Stalin) "Division into races is division of men according to hereditary physical characteristics. . . . The affirmation of the racists that

The division of society into classes is a historically limited phenomenon... 41
The division of society into exploiter and exploited did not exist in primitive society and under socialism it definitively ceases to exist. The appearance of classes is directly bound up with private ownership of the means of production, which makes possible the exploitation of man by man. For a certain stage in development, the division of society into classes was inevitable and historically necessary.

As long as human work still produced so little that there was only a small surplus over the necessary existence-level, stressed Engels, growth of the forces of production, spread of commerce, the development of state and law, the creation of art and science, were possible only through a greater division of labor, the basis of which is that great division of labor between the masses which are engaged solely with physical work and the privileged few who direct work, carry on commerce, run government and later are active in science and art ... When the development of the forces of production has made necessary the replacement of private by social property and the elimination of relations of exploitation, then there is no further reason for the existence of classes. The retention of classes is not only superfluous but also becomes a hindrance to the further development of society. (157–158).

The Marxist-Leninist theory of classes and class-war provides the key 42
for understanding the state ... ; it explains on a scientific basis its essence, its coming-to-be and development, the dissolution of one state by another, and the inevitability of the withering away of the state.... Earlier in the history of mankind, during the classless tribal society, there was no state. The function of administering social affairs was exercised by the society itself. As, however, ... society split into inimical classes, ... the exploiter-classes took a dominant position. So the state came to be a machine for maintaining the rule of one class over another. With the help of this machine, the economically ruling class assures itself of a profitable social order ... (162)

one race is superior to another is disproved by science as well as by the experience of world-history which proves that all people on earth are capable of creating cultural values and the measure of their contribution to world culture is not determined by their color or cranial characteristics but by the peculiarities of their historical development." (156–157)

43   History has seen three *basic types* of exploiter-states: slave-holding, feudal
and bourgeois.... A new, completely different state is the socialist state
where the working class and all workers, who form the majority or
totality of society, are in power... The monarchy is distinguished...
from the republic by the *structural form* of the highest organ of power.
(163) There are diverse forms of the bourgeois state: democratic republic,
constitutional monarchy, openly fascist dictatorship, etc. In all cases,
however, it remains a tool of the bourgeoisie, i.e., above all, a tool for
repressing the working masses. (164)

44   Reactionary ideologists... try to present class-war as a disruption of
progress, as a dangerous deviation from the normal course of social
development.... In reality, class-war not only does not disrupt progress
but is, on the contrary, the motive force of social development. Class-war
runs through the whole history of exploiter-society. Its creative and
progressive importance is evident under the conditions of the 'peaceful'
and evolutionary development of every formation. (165) The conflict of
oppressed classes plays an enormous role in political life.... The role of
class-war as the motive force of development is particularly clear in the
exploiter-society during a period of dissolution of one social-economic
formation by another, i.e. in an era of social revolution. (166)

45   The conflict between the forces of production and the relations of production – which is the economic basis of social revolution – grows up
slowly and gradually in the course of the development of the old means of
production. For the resolution of this conflict, there must be a radical
upheaval in the dominant relations of production and this can never come
through gradual changes. The interests of the dominant classes are
inseparably bound up with these relations even when they do not correspond to the state of the forces of production.... No single exploiter-class
has given up or will freely give up its property, the source of its privileged
status.... And, finally, the superannuated ruling class is not simply a
small group of people..., but an organized force which has been in
power for some time... Therefore, the dissolution of these relations
through other, newer ones, comes not through evolution but through
revolution which removes all hindrances from the path of the development
of new economic relations and, above all, the political domination of the
old classes.... The basic question of revolution is the question of power

and its going over into the hands of the class which incarnates the new relations of production. (166–167)

Chapter 6

THE ROLE OF THE POPULAR MASSES AND OF THE INDIVIDUAL IN HISTORY

The daily work of millions of simple men, who are developing production,   46 not only provides society with all that is necessary for its existence, but also creates the material basis for the continuing change of social-economic formations, ... for the progress of mankind. ... The masses also play a major role in political life. The development of society and, more importantly, of social revolution is impossible without their political activity, ... In 'peaceful' periods of history the role of the popular masses in the political life of the exploiter-society is not as evident. The ruling classes ... try to reduce the political activity of the popular masses to a minimum. (182–184) The Marxist doctrine on the decisive role of the popular masses in history arouses in the workers a deep sense of responsibility for the nature of society. It shows them that one must not await a 'savior', that the only hero who can free the people from oppression and bring society into harmony with the wishes of the majority of mankind is the workers themselves. (817)

Marxist theory, even though it attributes the decisive role in history to the   47 popular masses, recognizes – at the same time – the activity of eminent men, of the leader, and shows that they have a necessary function in society. ... Each social class can rule in society only through a definite organisation. But every class-organisation must, in order to work, have leadership. This is true for parties, for other social organisations and for the state. The leader elaborates the policy of the class, formulates it, organizes its realization, and directs the activities of thousands and millions of men. (187–188) The course of history is determined by the fight of larger social groups, e.g., classes and masses. The role of great men in history can only be understood in function of class-war ... The activity of all men, including the great ones, takes place under specific social conditions. These social conditions determine the objective laws of the development and tasks which stand before society. Prominent men who are put forward by progressive classes are great because they – better and earlier – understood these tasks. (188–189) Such an interpretation of history is irreconcilable with that hero worship and the fear of a prominent leader to whom is attributed some sort of supernatural accomplishments and miracles. (191) One must deal with the activity of the popular masses in their development.... The general direction of change since the division of society into classes shows an increase in the influence of the working masses on the development of the various aspects of social life and, above all, on politics. (194–195)

Chapter 7

SOCIAL PROGRESS

48   In general, the development of society runs in an ascending line; it is progressive, a movement from lower to higher. Such is the conclusion drawn by Marxist theory from a scientific analysis of the historical process, based not on subjective hopes and wishes but on strictly objective criteria.... The objective criteria are different in the various domains of life.[1] In order to judge the forward motion of the whole society and not of its separate parts, it is necessary ... to have general, universal criteria. Such a criterion, i.e. a measuring-stick of the progressive character of one or another formation, is for Marxism–Leninism the development of the forces of production. Progressive is that formation which includes new possibilities for the development of forces of production, which guarantees a higher rate of growth and reaches a higher level. (200)

49   Why do Marxists attribute priority precisely to this criterion? Above all, because the development of the forces of production is the direct measuring-stick of progress in a domain as important as the production of man's vital needs.... The development of the forces of production determines the degree of man's mastery over nature.... Progress in other domains of social life (social relations, culture, etc.) depends on the development of the forces of production. With the development of the forces of production, there is an increase of the culture of workers, of their consciousness and their organisation. (200–201)

[1] Public health and material well-being; average life-span; culture; literacy rate; education; number of schools, libraries, scientific institutions; theater.

While Marxist theory maintains that the history of society is a movement 50
along an ascending line, it at the same time views it in the fullness of its
complexities and contradictions. But, history is not to be conceived as a
harmonious, uninterrupted and unimpeded forward motion of society....
Science has already collected many facts which show that in the history
of different lands there have been many periods of standstill, reverse and
disappearance of civilisations. ... In reality, such facts only evidence the
contradictory and uneven character of social progress under the conditions
of exploiter-society. (206)

One form of this contradictoriness is the fact that, under the conditions 51
of exploiter-domination, those countries which broke through to go
forward, overcame and suffocated (and often shoved backwards) condemned civilisations and based their own growth on the ruins of the
latter. In this way the forward motion of mankind went on for a long
time on a very small front and not in a closed formation of all lands and
peoples.... Further, every progress of one – even in one and the same
society – means reverse for another, the freeing of one class means new
oppression for another. The development of the various sides of social
life also remains very uneven. (206)

What are the basic traits of social progress under socialism? First of all, 52
not just a handful of the chosen, but rather all workers profit from it....
There is no privileged class here. All of the fruits of progress fall to the
workers.... Under socialism, progress out of capitalism is not made at
the expense of some lands, areas and nations but by the common front
of all socialist nations and lands ... The more progressive help the backward ... Under socialism social progress will be ever more the result of
the conscious and planned activity of man ... The most important
particularity and a mighty factor of progress under socialism is the direct,
active and conscious participation of the great popular masses in the
construction of the new society. (209–210)

THE POLITICAL ECONOMY OF CAPITALISM

Note: The economic theory of Marxism-Leninism contains numerous sections which have to do with technical-organizational details of commercial economics, e.g. money, production factors, functional elements of capital and of reproduction, etc. These parts are omitted in what follows: we have concentrated on the social-critical theses.

Chapter 8

PRE-MONOPOLISTIC CAPITALISM

53　Capitalist production can come to be only under two conditions. It requires the concentration of the basic means of production in the hands of the capitalists. Further, it is necessary that all or most of society be without means of production. This forces those who have nothing but their working hands to serve the capitalists as salaried workers in order not to starve. (219) Marx clearly saw the antagonistic character of the relationship between work and capital as the axle around which the whole capitalist economic system turned. His investigation of plus-value provided a creative, scientific explanation of the process of exploitation of the worker by the capitalists. (226)

CAPITALIST EXPLOITATION

54　Marx begins with the simple and well-known fact that the capitalists first buy the things necessary for production and then sell the products of their factories for more than they originally paid. (226) The question arises: how can the owner of money, the capitalist, draw from the circuit a greater value even though he buys and sells the wares at their real value? Marx answers this question which was unsolvable for bourgeois political economy. It appears that this is possible because the owner of money finds on the market a very peculiar type of merchandise, the use of which is the source of new value. This merchandise is work. (227)

55　What is the value of work? The value of all merchandise is measured by the amount of work necessary for its production. Work exists in the form of the living worker who needs a certain amount of provisions for himself and his family. The time necessary to produce these provisions determines the value of the work. (227) The value of work is paid but this value is by far less than that which the capitalist can extract from the work: this difference, the unpaid work, falls to the capitalist or – more exactly – to the capitalist class.... Thus, the salaried worker makes, during a part of his work-time, the product which is necessary for his own preservation. This Marx calls *necessary work-time*: and the work done then is called the *necessary work*. During the rest of his work-time – the plus-work-time – the worker creates, through his *plus-work* plus-value. *Plus-value* is the value which is created by the work of the worker over and above his own existence and which the capitalist gratuitously appropriates. (228)

The capitalists try to hold the salary to its physical minimum. The working   56
class fights to improve its standard of living. Therefore, the motion of salary is essentially dependent on the class-war of the proletariat, on its being organized, and on the degree of its opposition to capital. The fight of the working class for the improvement of working conditions and the elevation of its standard of living – but with preservation of private ownership of means of production and political power in the hands of the bourgeoisie – can ameliorate its lot. Nevertheless this fight does not affect the foundations of capitalist society and cannot free workers from capitalist wage-slavery. (231)

Profit is the motive force and main object of every capitalist. For the   57
capitalist, production is only a means of making profit. As concerns the popular masses, they are taken into account in capitalist economy only insofar as they are an unavoidable prerequisite for the making of profit: outside of this calculation, the question of use or abuse of the masses loses all sense for the capitalists. (233) Bourgeois economists rate capitalist profit as the best stimulus for technical progress and the unlimited growth of production. They pass over in silence the fact that capitalist profit is the result of the exploitation and wearing down of work. They do not say that the subordination of production to the principle of capitalist profit is not only the stimulus but also the barrier of capitalist production.... Capitalists...often limit production, stop technological progress and destroy a series of products in order to raise profit-margins. Moreover, capitalist monopolies engender wars, bring immense misery to mankind, and all this in the name of profits! (236)

ECONOMIC CRISES OF OVER-PRODUCTION

58 The efforts of the capitalists for limitless expansion of production while consumption is confined within the narrow limits of the creditable demand of the masses, is solved by expanding production mainly in the field of means of production. . . . The expansion of production under such conditions – since the production of consumer goods is limited by the low income of the masses – leads to periodic economic crises of over-production. (242)

59 The economic crisis is an over-production of goods, an increase of difficulties in selling them, decrease in prices, a rapid decrease in production. During a crisis, employment falls sharply, wages fall, credit disappears and many small capitalists are ruined. (243)

60 Crises evidence the ever increasing imbalance between bourgeois relations of production and the character of modern forces of production. Crises of over-production are clear indications of the limited character of the capitalist means of production, of their inability to provide growing room for the forces of production. The crises show that contemporary society can provide incomparably more products for the amelioration of the life of all workers if the means of production are used not for gaining capitalist profits but for the satisfaction of the needs of all members of society. (244)

THE UNIVERSAL LAW AND HISTORICAL TREND OF CAPITALIST ACCUMULATION

61 The more rapid growth of constant capital in comparison to variable [1] capital leads to a relative decline in capitalist production's need for the work of the worker even though the number of workers increases with the development of capitalism. Technological progress under capitalism condemns millions of men to unemployment. . . . The bigger the industrial reserve army, the worse is the situation of the portion of the working class which has work since the capitalist can fire unsuitable and recalcitrant workers, knowing that he can always find replacements for them. (245)

62 The worsening of the living conditions of the workers is accentuated

[1] Constant capital is made up of investments in machines, buildings and means of transport, while variable capital is that spent for wages. (229)

during economic crises of over-production when lay-offs increase, wages decrease, and the ruin of small and medium industrialists is accelerated. ...A worsening of the situation of the worker can also take place if wages rise some. Higher work-rates raise the need for better food, medical care, etc. And if these increased needs are not satisfied – or only partially so – the workers' situation grows worse and their need increases even though wages have risen somewhat. Even more obvious is the relative worsening of the situation of the worker – a phenomenon specific to capitalism – due to the decrease in his share of the national product.... Increase in national wealth leads necessarily under capitalism to an increase in the social inequality between the capitalists and the workers. The tendency toward a worsening of the situation of the worker during the development of capitalism – a fact discovered by Marx – continues today. (245–246)

The Marxist thesis on the tendency toward worsening of the situation of the working class is often presented as a dogma according to which capitalism, from year to year and decade to decade, brings an absolute decline in the lot of the worker. Yet Marx enunciated this thesis not as an uninterrupted process but in the sense of a *tendency* of capitalism which prevails irregularly in different areas and during different periods with deviations and interruptions, and against which other factors work. One of the other factors is the fight of the working class for wage-increase and amelioration of the work conditions. . . . The workers of many lands have been able to improve their situation ... It is clear that this does not in the least refute Marxism. (246–247)   **63**

The internal laws of capitalist production result in the elimination of the weaker capitalists by the stronger.... There comes a moment when the transformation of the decisive means of production into social property is not only possible but also necessary because the contradiction between the social character of production and the private-capitalist mode of ownership has reached its ultimate expression. The accumulation of capital creates not only the objective but also the subjective prerequisites for the transition from capitalism to socialism.... The proletariat rises ... ever more resolutely against capital. The working class directs its efforts toward changing capitalist property into social property. (247–248)   **64**

Chapter 9

IMPERIALISM AS THE HIGHEST AND LAST STAGE OF CAPITALISM

65   Near the end of the nineteenth century, capitalism entered a new stage of its development, the imperialist stage.... Lenin defined it as follows: "Imperialism is a distinct historical stage of capitalism. Its distinctness is triple; imperialism is: (1) monopolistic capitalism; (2) parasitic or rotting capitalism; (3) dying capitalism." (249)

MONOPOLISTIC CAPITALISM

66   Lenin indicates five basic economic traits of imperialism: "(1) Concentration of production and of capital, which has reached such a high degree of development that it creates monopolies which play a decisive role in economic life; (2) Merger of bank-capital with industry-capital and the coming-to-be of an oligarchy of finance on the basis of 'finance-capital'; (3) the export of capital – as distinguished from the export of merchandise – gains in importance; (4) international, monopolistic bands of capitalists who divide the world are formed; and (5) the territorial division of the earth by the large capitalist powers is completed." (249)

67   A monopoly is a union or band of capitalists who concentrate in their hands the production and distribution of a significant portion (or the totality) of the production of one or more branches of the economy. (250) A small group of large owners of *finance-capital* have become an oligarchy of finance and have seized control of the key-positions of the economy in capitalist lands. (255)

68   The export of capital is investing abroad in order to take possession of the plus-value of the workers of other lands.... Capital export becomes necessary when capitalism has become 'too ripe' in one country. (256)

69   "The countries which export capital", wrote Lenin, "have in a metaphorical sense divided the world. But, finance-capital leads to the direct division of the world".... Under capitalism the world market, like the internal market, is divided 'according to capital', 'according to strength'. But, the power-balance of the monopolies is in constant change. Every

22

monopoly fights constantly to increase its share of the world's wealth. International monopolies are unstable. They cannot and do not survive strong competition. (257–258)

In addition to the division of the world by the capitalist gangs of various   70
lands and in close conjunction with it, there is the territorial division of the world by the imperialist states. (258) The territorial division of the world was (at the end of the century, *H.F.*) completed. To seek new colonies or spheres of influence was now possible only by taking them away from another colonial power. Colonies became ever more important for the imperialist states. There followed an era of conflict and of new division of the already divided world. The monopolies, which ruled at home, now sought to conquer all other lands and to subject them to the most brutal exploitation. (259) Lenin showed that the capitalism of the beginning of the twentieth century had become "a world-system of colonial oppression and financial strangulation of the vast majority by a handful of 'developed' countries". (260)

PARASITIC CAPITALISM

Often the monopolies artificially limit the production of one or another   71
product in order to maintain a high price and profit. This is, of course, a great obstacle to technological progress. (261) Parasitism in the imperialist era is clearly expressed in the existence of a rich class – people who own stocks and live by 'cutting coupons'. (263)

Political reaction. Capitalism conquered feudalism under the banner of   72
freedom, equality and fraternity. Bourgeois democracy is fitting as the form of political domination for pre-monopolistic capitalism. Things changed with the transition to imperialism. The formation of monopolies meant the transition from free enterprise to a state of domination and force. Monopolies became the rulers of economic life. As lords of the economy, the monopolies also tried to acquire political power and, thereby, put the bourgeois state under their purvey. With power once in their hands, the monopolies ever oftener set aside the methods of bourgeois democracy and turned to political reaction. The rottenness of capitalism is clearly evidenced in political reaction.... A characteristic example of the gains of political reaction is *fascism* which is the terroristic

23

dictatorship of the monopolistic bourgeoisie and of the great land-owners. (263–264)

73 *"Worker-aristocracy"*. A characteristic symptom of the foulness of capitalism is the systematic corruption by the monopolistic bourgeoisie of certain workers. The imperialists are interested in drawing out of the proletariat certain privileged groups of workers. (264)

DYING CAPITALISM

74 In the period of imperialism are developed the material prerequisites for the transition to a higher social-economic system, i.e. to socialism.... Imperialism falls under the weight of its own crimes. The working masses, which rise up to fight for the victory of the socialist revolution, conquer it. (268)

75 Therefore, imperialism is dying capitalism since it expresses the ultimate aggravation of the contradictions of capitalism; especially of the basic contradiction of capitalism – that between the social character of pro-duction and the private-capitalist form of ownership.... On this basis, all the contradictions of capitalism are aggravated, the most important of which are: the contradiction between the oppressed peoples of de-pendent countries and the imperialist powers exploiting them; the contradictions between the imperialist powers themselves. The aggravation of these contradictions brings the downfall of capitalism and the coming of the socialist revolution nearer. (167)

THE BEGINNING OF THE GENERAL CRISIS OF CAPITALISM

76 Under imperialism, capitalism enters directly into the era of its general crisis.... As seen in Chapter 8, periodic economic crises are proper to capitalism ... The general crisis is marked by the fact that it is the all-inclusive crisis of capitalism as a social system. This is a lasting state marked by the rapid disintegration of capitalism and the sapping of all its internal forces (economic, political, ideological).... During the general crisis, capitalism is no longer able to keep the peoples under its control and one by one they throw off the yoke of capitalism and stride the path to socialism. (269)

24

The political weakening of capitalism evokes a further and stronger revival   77
of the reactionary essence of the imperialistic bourgeoisie.... The
beginning of the general crisis was also marked by an increase in the
aggressivity of imperialism and a further aggravation of the contradictions between the imperialist powers and between a handful of
imperialist robbers and the rest of the world.... The increasingly uneven
development of the imperialist countries results in an even more bitter
fight for raw materials and markets.... The most aggressive groups of
the monopolistic bourgeoisie seek escape from the crisis in the use of
naked force and, above all, in a new world war. (271–272)

Chapter 10

IMPERIALISM TODAY

The Second World War was not only incapable of saving capitalism from   78
its general crisis but, on the contrary, lead to a great aggravation and
deepening of this crisis and opened a new stage in it.... What are the
characteristics of the new stage in the general crisis of capitalism? *First,*
an essential modification of the balance of forces between the socialist
system and the imperialist system resulting, above all, from the defection
from capitalism of a series of countries of Europe and Asia and the
transformation of socialism into a world-system. *Second,* the greatly
advance degeneration of the colonial system of imperialism and the
aggravation of contradictions between the imperialist powers and the
colonial, semi-colonial and ex-colonial lands. *Third,* the growth of new
contradictions within the imperialist camp, especially between the USA
and the other developed capitalist countries resulting from the strengthened expansion of American imperialism and its fight for world domination. *Fourth,* the deepening and spread of class-oppositions in countries
of developed capitalism. (273) ... Thus it is now much more evident that
the general crisis of capitalism is, above all, a crisis of the imperialist
system ... (274)

The imperialists are not happy with this historical change. With the war   79
only just ended they began a feverish arms race to prepare a new world-
wide conflagration, and they began the 'cold war' against the socialist
countries. The new stage in the general crisis of capitalism is an era of the

increased aggressivity of imperialism and of an increase in that danger of war which now hangs over the world. (274)

80 The source of all of these contradictions in contemporary imperialism is the aggravation of the basic contradiction of capitalism, i.e. that between the social character of production and the private character of ownership. The limitation of the imperialist sphere of exploitation, the aggravation of class-antagonisms, and the contradictions between the imperialist powers – all this created new difficulties for the further development of the forces of production under continuance of private property and of anarchy in production. Growth of production more and more clearly requires freedom from the chains of capitalistic property. (275)

GOVERNMENT-MONOPOLY CAPITALISM

81 With the recent deepening and aggravation of these contradictions... the monopolies could not assure domination with the earlier methods. Whence came transition to new, government-monopoly forms of capitalist domination. The transition of monopoly capitalism to government-monopoly capitalism means the joining of the power of the capitalist monopolies with the power of the state wherein the state becomes subservient to large capitalist groups. (274) A characteristic trait of modern government-monopoly capitalism is the formation of an important governmental market in the form of government contracts, financing of the purchase of surpluses, etc.... This leads to an increase of the role of government finance in the economy.... At the beginning of the century in the USA and England only a small percentage of the national income was raised by taxes; in 1956–1958 this figure was 25%. (279)

82 An important factor in the development of government-monopoly capitalism was the depression of 1929–1933.... Since this time, government-monopoly anti-crisis measures have become an integral function of the imperialist state.[1] (276–277)

83 Government-monopoly capitalism also brings an increase in government ownership. (279) A characteristic of government-monopoly capitalism is

---

[1] Public works, surplus-buying, 'dumping', etc.

its active interference in conflicts between workers and employers and its efforts to stifle the unrest of the masses with force. (281)

MILITARIZATION OF THE ECONOMY

Militarization of the economy is indissolubly bound up with the increase   84
of government-monopolistic tendencies of imperialist powers. (281) The big corporations try by all means to solve the selling problem through governmental demand for war materials. They are very interested in armaments which guarantee their super-profits. . . . It would be, however, false to try to explain the militarization of the economy by purely economic causes. It is inseparable from the general line of both the internal and foreign policies of the imperialist states. . . . These policies are not only criminal but also, in the end, useless, since they do not solve the basic contradictions of modern capitalism. (282)

HAS CAPITALISM BEEN FREED FROM ECONOMIC CRISES?

After the depression of 1929–1933 and especially after the Second World   85
War, monopoly-capital with the help of the state created a whole system of anti-crisis measures. These measures form a specific portion of the mechanism of government-monopoly capitalism. The most important anti-crisis measures are enormous orders and purchases of weapons and strategic raw materials . . . Governmental regulation of credit also becomes very important . . . The proponents of government-monopolist capitalism make much of these and similar measures and maintain that, with their help, capitalism has been cured from the disease of crises and that a continuous growth of capitalist production has been assured. (292–293) Doubtlessly, government-monopoly capitalism can influence · the form, consequences and character of isolated economic crises. The great monopolies are in a position to use the enormous financial power of the state as a damper on the spontaneous outbreak of crises and in order to soften the blow. (294) Even if the representatives of government-monopoly capitalism have a certain influence on the course of the crisis, they do not eliminate the causes of the crisis but rather drive the disease underground where it serves as basis for further crises. . . . Changes in the apparent characteristics of crises – such as have been evident recently, especially in the USA – offer no proof that all economic crises under

government-monopoly capitalism will have this form.... One thing is perfectly clear: as long as there is the contradiction between the social character of production and the capitalist (private) character of ownership, i.e. as long as capitalism exists, the economic crises will be unavoidable. (295)

THE DEEPENING AND SPREAD OF CLASS-CONFLICTS

86 *Working class and capital.* With the development of the general crisis of capitalism the exploitation of the working class necessarily intensifies and its situation becomes worse. This is evident, above all, in the extraordinary intensification of work and the consequent increase of work accidents and diseases as result of over-exertion.... It is true that recently there has been an almost universal increase in the nominal earnings of the worker. But, this is compensated for by inflation and rise in taxes. In the end, real wages in capitalist countries have risen very little or not at all. (298)

87 In addition, the instability of the position of the worker ... has been increased as never before in modern capitalism. It is a question not only of a fear of crises and massive unemployment but also of constant fear of accidents, illness or over-exertion leading to loss of the ability to work. Early invalidity affects the worker like a landslide. (299) Thereby, the tendency to worsen the situation of the working class is still characteristic of capitalism. Granted, the working class (or some parts of it) in some capitalist countries has, during the last ten or fifteen years, partially improved its situation. This does not mean that capitalism's basic tendency has changed. The main cause (of this improvement) is that there were better conditions after the war for the fight of the working class (mainly due to the successes of the socialist countries) which hardened its resistance to the monopolies. (300)

88 *The other classes of society.* In addition to the working class and the capitalists, there are in bourgeois society other classes and social levels: peasants, petty bourgeoisie of the cities, intelligentsia, and white-collar workers. In numbers and in importance for the life of society, these so-called middle classes are an important force.... The ideologists of the reactionary bourgeoisie maintain that there is in progress a gradual widening of the "middle classes" at the expense of all other classes.

Society will supposedly become more and more a unitarian "middle-class society" whose situation will constantly improve. (301) Facts fully refute this propagandistic interpretation. In particular, they show that the development of government-monopoly capitalism directly ruins a significant portion of the "middle-classes". (302)

This is especially true of the independent small producer (the so-called *old* 89 middle-class, i.e. a sort of left-over of the pre-capitalist methods of production and distribution), i.e. peasants, artisans, small manufacturers, etc. ... It is well known that an ever smaller number of smaller merchants and producers are "independent". (302)

While the middle-class of small producers is being constantly ruined and 90 expelled, the intelligentsia, white-collar workers and other middle-classes – the so-called *new* "middle-classes" – undergo the opposite process. Technological progress, together with growth of the administrative apparatus, leads to a rapid increase in the number and specific influence of white-collar workers, technicians, scientists, bookkeepers, advertisers, distributors and, finally, the press, teachers and artists, etc. But, the situation of these growing social levels worsens, above all, because the work of the intelligentsia becomes widespread and, therefore, less valuable and less privileged. (302)

When speaking of "middle-classes" one must remember that they include 91 such social groups as serve the interests of the reactionary bourgeoisie, e.g., higher government officials, business executives, privileged groups of the intelligentsia, etc. (303)

The reactionary theoreticians confuse ... the question of the ruling class 92 when they maintain that the influence of capitalists in modern bourgeois society is on the decline. The capitalists, they say, ... are losing their dominant position; without any revolution ... they are retiring from the social scene. (304) Widespread in bourgeois propaganda of the last decade is also the theory of the "managerial revolution", according to which the real power over the economy (and, therefore, over politics) is supposedly ... passing from those who 'formally' own to those who factually direct ... Now, the role of the capitalist in production has been changing – the owners abdicate their last useful function and are represented by clerks. This is only one more argument for dispossessing capital and for

29

the transition to socialism. This changes nothing in the exploiter-nature of capitalism. The owner still has the real power over production.... The engineers and clerks of a monopoly cannot dispossess the owner, while the owner can – as has been the case for hundreds of years – fire the engineers and clerks and/or dictate to them. Naturally, there are senior clerks of the trusts who really have extensive power... But, in reality, they are capitalists as well, except that they draw the profit in the form of a salary. (305)

THE LAST RUNG IN CAPITALISM'S HISTORICAL LADDER

93 Once begun, the general crisis of capitalism proceeds with gathering momentum to the full collapse of capitalism. The analysis of the situation of contemporary capitalism and of the basic laws of its development warrants the conclusion that all the measures which are taken by the monopolistic bourgeoisie to save capitalism cannot bring relief from the ever-worsening contradictions but, on the contrary, will lead to further breakdown. (306–307)

94 In the fight against the socialist lands the imperialist camp has brought all its methods into play... As answer to the violent attacks of the imperialists ... the socialist camp stands fast. Also without success are the efforts of the imperialists to rebuild or maintain their degenerating colonial empire.... Just as vain have been the efforts of the monopolistic bourgeoisie to hold down the class-war of the workers in the key-countries of capitalism. (307)

95 From all of this one can conclude that the greatest difficulties of contemporary monopoly capitalism are not behind but before it. The social character of production requires ever more categorically the abolition of the private ownership of the means of production and the dissolution of capitalism by socialism. (308)

THEORY AND TACTICS OF THE INTERNATIONAL COMMUNIST MOVEMENT

After a profound analysis of the economics of capitalism, Marx and   96
Engels came to the conclusion that in the womb of this society lie the
seeds of its downfall and of its replacement by another social formation,
socialism. But the founders of Marxism were not content to indicate just
the basis trend of further development: in the proletariat, the working
class, they discovered the leading social force which was called upon to
achieve the great social change, i.e. to destroy capitalism and to build
socialism. (310)

Chapter 11

THE WORLD-WIDE, HISTORICAL MISSION OF THE WORKING CLASS

On what did Marx and Engels base their prediction on the world-wide,   97
historical mission of the working class? First, on the fact that the working
class, as the most exploited class in capitalist society, is by reason of its
living conditions the most consistent and uncompromising enemy of the
capitalist order. Vital interests force the worker into an uncompromising
fight with capitalism. (310) Second, they saw that the worker is, by his
whole position in the process of production, bound up not with the past
but with the future of the whole of society. . . . Above all, this means that
the development of the material basis of capitalism – i.e. heavy industry –
. . . leads to a numerical increase of workers and to an increase of their
role in the life of society. It further means that the interests and the efforts
of the working class coincide with the basic direction in the development
of the forces of production. . . . When Marx and Engels drew the conclusion that it is precisely the working class which is called upon to
destroy capitalism and to construct socialism, they were operating on the
fact that it is the only class which has the fighting qualities which are
necessary for the realization of such an immense historical task. (310–311)

The working class has, above all, the advantage of size. It is one of the   98
largest and most rapidly increasing classes of capitalist society. . . . The
working class is – thanks to the circumstances of its life and work –

capable of extraordinary organization. Work in large-scale production produces in the worker such qualities as a collective spirit, a penchant for strict discipline, common action, mutual help and aid. These qualities are useful not only for work but also for the fight. (311–312)

99   The working class is the most fight-capable and revolutionary class of society. And, therefore, it is entrusted with the mission of liquidating capitalism and establishing socialism. The working class is called upon to definitively destroy the roots of social inequality – private ownership of the means of production, which causes the split of society into rich and poor, exploiter and exploited, oppressor and oppressed. The fulfilment of this task is the sole path to the freeing of society from poverty and lawlessness, from political and national oppression, from militarism and war. (312–313)

THE COMMUNITY OF INTERESTS OF THE WORKING CLASS AND ALL WORKERS

100   The strength of the working class lies not only in its own numerical strength, its consciousness and organisation, but also in its community of interests with the vital interests of all other workers. This community of interests has deep roots in capitalist reality. Under the yoke of capitalism, it is not only the worker who suffers, but also the broad masses of the peasants, the petty bourgeoisie of the city, the intelligentsia and administrative workers. . . . Irrespective of the attitude of these other levels of workers toward the basic goals of the socialist movement, there are not a few important concrete tasks for which they can and do fight together with the workers. Among these tasks, the primary is the defence of direct economic interests against the attacks of the monopolies, the preservation of peace, of national independence, of democracy, etc. . . . (317)

101   The vast majority of the *peasantry*, which in many countries is the largest population group, suffer even today under either the remains of feudalism or the yoke of capitalism or a mixture of the two. Can capitalism solve the problems which bother the peasantry? No, because capitalist development can bring only further ruin, loss of land and proletarization of the village. Only socialism solves the problems which face the working peasant because it frees him from the yoke both of the land-owner and of the

capitalist and opens before him perspectives so vast that he could never before even have dreamed of them. The same is true of the *urban petty bourgeoisie*. (318)

A quite numerous and growing level of capitalist society is made up of those who do mental work: clerks, technicians, teachers, doctors, artists, etc. Many of them earlier had formed a privileged social group but now the vast majority are exploited and oppressed by the ruling oligarchy. Only socialism can free them from this oppression by opening undreamed of reaches for the maturing of culture, and by freeing them from the debasing influence of the gold-bags. (318) 102

There are then, today, very favorable conditions for the union of the working class with the other social levels which are resisting the reactionary bourgeoisie. The working class is called upon to play a special role in such a partnership, the role of the leader and chief.... The working class is not trying to gain privileges at the expense of the other classes and levels of society. On the contrary, the leadership of the working masses implies new duties for the working class... (319) 103

INTERNATIONALISM

The first definitely international class is the working class, the prole- 104
tariat.... Workers have no private property, which splits men, and no interests which could cause conflict with the workers of other lands and nationalities. On the contrary, the basic interest of the workers of all lands – the end of capitalist domination – is the same. This interest consolidates the international forces of capital against them and makes internationalism not only possible but necessary for the worker: it is the inescapable condition of their victorious fight for socialism and Communism.... Without internationalism, without unity of the efforts of the workers of all lands, one will not be able to defeat the world-bourgeoisie and build the new society. (320–321)

THE WORKING CLASS AS THE HOPE OF PROGRESSIVE HUMANITY

The eminent fighting qualities of the working class make it the vanguard 105
of all progressive mankind. In many lands the working class has over-thrown the bourgeoisie and taken the lead in society. In contradistinction

to the oppressed classes of the past – the slaves and serfs – this class will not leave the historical scene once they have played the role of main battering-ram, overturned the old rulers and broken the old order. Before it, remains the task of constructing the new society, which cannot be entrusted to someone else. To fulfil this task not only the properties of a fighter are required but also the capacity for creative activity in all domains of the life of society: in economy, culture, politics and military affairs. The capacity for creative accomplishments must be objectively present in the working class to a higher degree than in any other class in history since no other has had such a great historical mission. Both in depth and extent, the social transformation from capitalism to socialism surpasses all other social revolutions. History has demonstrated that the working class fully possesses the capacity for creative activity which is necessary for the construction of the new society. (329–330)

106 For the accomplishment of its grandiose task of the construction of the new society the working class draws to itself the best scientists and technicians – the intelligentsia which grew up in the old society – and, at the same time, forms its own, new intelligentsia which is drawn from the working class and the working peasantry. In addition, there grows up in the course of socialist construction and the movement toward Communist society a drastic need to make the whole working class an educated class, i.e. to form them with middle and higher education, higher culture and specialized knowledge in all branches of social production. (330)

Note: Chapter 12 deals with "The Great October Revolution as the Basic Change-Over in the History of Mankind". We omit it here since its general theses (on revolutionary strategy) are treated in the following chapter.

Chapter 13

THE MARXIST-LENINIST PARTY AND ITS ROLE IN THE CLASS-WAR OF THE WORKER

107 When Marx and Engels scientifically established the historical role of the working class, they simultaneously saw that for the transformation of capitalist society to socialism the proletariat necessarily needed a self-sufficient political party. (349) Marx and Engels drew (from the experience of the League of Communists and of the First International, *H.F.*) many

important conclusions on the role of the revolutionary party of the working class, on its organization and policies. Under new historical conditions Lenin developed these conclusions into a structured doctrine on the party. He established the leadership role of the party in the workers' movement, formulated the principles of organization and the norms of its internal life, as well as the basic principles of its policies and tactics. This doctrine is one of Lenin's very important contributions to Marxism. (349–350)

Of all organizations founded by the proletariat, only the political party 108 can correctly express the basic interests of the working class and lead it to full victory. With the help of only unions, cooperatives and such organizations, the worker could never bring capitalism down and construct socialist society. For this, is necessary an organization of a higher type, one which is not content with satisfaction of the momentary needs of the workers but rather works to bring the working class to power in order to accomplish the revolutionary transformation of society. (350) However, not every party which pretends to lead the working class is able to accomplish this task. This is proved by experience with the social-democratic parties ... With the help of the opportunistic leaders of the social-democracy the bourgeoisie was able to significantly influence these parties and to "tame" them so that they are hardly distinguishable from normal bourgeois parliamentary opposition. Consequently, the social-democratic parties, which had aroused the hopes of the working class, lost the ability to organize and direct the revolutionary movement of the workers. This was especially clear in the extreme aggravation of all social contradictions which the era of imperialism brought with it. Objective reality and the interests of the proletariat demanded the immediate creation of a worker's party of a new type. (351)

The main characteristic of the party of a new type is its uncompromising 109 attitude toward capitalism. Communists fight actively for its dissolution, for the revolutionary transformation of capitalist society, and are of the opinion that the unavoidable condition of such a transformation is the conquering of political power by the working class and the establishment of the dictatorship of the proletariat. And from this derives the Communists' lack of patience with any form of opportunism which, in practice, means compromise with capitalism. (351–352)

110   Communist Parties do not act on impulse or blindly, but are lead by the revolutionary theory of Marxism-Leninism which scientifically expresses the basic interests of the working class. The Party is a free union of like-minded people who have banded together to realize the Marxist world-outlook and to fulfil the historical mission of the working class. The revolutionary character of the Party determines its organizational principles, its firmness, unanimity in action and elasticity of tactics. But the main strength of the Communist Parties is that they are not made up of lone wolves or small groups of professional revolutionaries but of the working masses with which the Parties are as closely bound up as possible and whose fight they try to lead. (352) The Communist Party is the vanguard of the working class, i.e. its progressive and conscious part which is able to lead the broad masses of workers with it in the fight for the destruction of capitalism and the construction of socialism. (352)

DEMOCRATIC CENTRALISM

111   The principles of the organizational structure of the Communist Party are determined by its role in the workers' movement and by the character of its goals and tasks.... Only a *centralized* leadership can unify all forces, lead them toward a goal and give unity to the separate actions of distinct workers and workers' groups.... But, the general will of the Party can only be built in a democratic way, i.e. collectively, in that different opinions and suggestions are expressed, a decision is made, and is binding on all.... Thus, the centralism of the Communist Party is a *democratic* centralism, i.e. based on the wills of the mass of Party members. (353–354)

112   In practice, *democratic centralism* means: electivity of all directive organs of the Party from top to bottom; periodic reports of the Party organizations to the Party organs; strict Party discipline and subordination of the minority to the majority; unconditional validity of the decisions of the higher organs for the lower. (354)

113   The inner life of the Party is so organized that the Communists take the most active part in practical work. This is the essence of Party democracy. For this reason, conditions are such that the Party members have the opportunity to discuss all questions, to check on the fulfilment of all decisions, to elect the leaders, and to know and check their activities. The

36

Communist Party does not reduce the inner democracy of the Party to participation in the election of the leaders ... The democracy of the Communist Party is a democracy of *active, unified operation*, i.e. where the members of the Party not only elect and discuss but also participate in the practical direction of Party work. (355)

However, the active participation of all Communists in the activity of the   114
Party does not diminish the importance of the leadership, and the role of the leaders who must have the necessary capabilities, knowledge and experience. The history of the workers' movement in various lands has shown that political parties can effectively operate only if they have stable groups of experienced, authoritative and influential leaders. Such men form the leadership core of the Party, its elected apparatus, which organizes the practical accomplishment of the objectives and guarantees the continuity of experience and tradition. The leaders of the Party are not superior to it but under its control. (355–356)

This unity of action by no means indicates that there cannot be differences   115
of opinion in the Party. Otherwise, the Party would not be a living but a dead organization. In daily work there can be differences of opinion on one question or another. This is unavoidable and permissible. Party discipline does not require that anyone give up his convictions if these do not contradict the principles of Marxism-Leninism. It does require that one submit himself to decisions already made and to their accomplishment, even if the Party member is not in agreement or had proposed another solution. Partly discipline also requires that internal Party questions not be discussed outside the Party. (357)

In the Party there are strict rules against those who do not submit them-   116
selves to decisions. The history of the Communist Party has seen examples of some people who, not being satisfied with the general line of the Party, formed their own group with its own discipline. Such groups, being against the majority, are called fractions. Fractionalism is a normal phenomenon ... in the opportunist parties. For Communist Parties – organizations of combat and action – the admission of fractions is equivalent to the abandon of the ideal unity and the leadership of the fight. Therefore, the formation of fractions is incompatible with the requirements of Party discipline. (357–358)

THE LIVING UNION OF THE PARTY WITH THE MASSES

117 The Communists can form a Party in the real sense of the word only if they are closely bound up with and supported by the masses.... How does the Party become a real leader? There is only one path: convince the masses that the Party correctly expresses their interests and defends them – with deeds rather than words, by its policies, initiative and devotion. The Party must gain the confidence and recognition of the broad masses through its work. (359)

118 Communists make an effort to work wherever there are workers. (359) It is natural that for the Communists the *mass organizations* – unions, organizations of women and children, cooperatives, etc. – have great importance.... Through these mass organizations, the Party unites itself more firmly with the workers. (360)

119 One can only lead ... and not run ahead of the masses – if one takes into consideration their experience and I.Q. ... But, taking into consideration their I.Q. is not conforming to it.... The Party can lead and teach the masses only when it itself has learned from the masses, i.e. closely and attentively studied what happens in popular practice and what is accepted in popular wisdom. To learn from the masses in order to teach the masses – this is the principle of Marxist-Leninist leadership, applied by all Communist Parties. (362)

MARXIST-LENINIST POLITICS AS A SCIENCE AND AN ART

120 One of the most important strengths of the Communist Parties is the fact that they base their policies on a scientific foundation. This means, above all, that the Communists can, in defending the interests of the working class, depend on Marxism-Leninism so that they are able to base their actions on a knowledge of the objective laws of social development and, in particular, of the laws of class-war. They consider in each period and each concrete situation the distribution of class-forces.... The measures constituting the activity of the Marxist-Leninist Party are not the result of an improvisation but the expression of the political line elaborated by the Party on the basis of a scientific analysis of the present stage of the fight, etc. In the language of politics one uses the terms tactics and strategy to designate this line. (363)

Lenin said of politics that it is not only a science but also an art. This 121
means that the political leadership must not only have a correct, scientific
analysis of the situation and, on this basis the elaboration of a correct
line, but also possess great ability and mastery – a veritable art – for its
implementation. (365–366) The science and art of political leadership also
shows itself in the ability to discover the main task on which special
efforts are to be concentrated. (368)

THE FIGHT AGAINST OPPORTUNISM OF THE RIGHT AND SECTARIANISM

The reactionary bourgeoisie has never given up trying to ruin the 122
Communist movement from within. It hopes to use internal Party
differences for its purposes and spreads opportunistic views among the
politically weak members of the Party ... Therefore, the fight for the
purity of the Marxist-Leninist world-outlook is an inviolable law of the
existence and development of Communist Parties. (369)

The ideologists of revisionism make it a point to "check up" or – more 123
correctly – to distort all the basic theses of Marxism-Leninism. ...
Ultimately, the theoretical and practical occupations of the revisionists
always tend toward reform or liquidation of the Party. ... Today,
however, the revisionists do not usually suggest out and out liquidation
of the Party. Under the banner of widening infra-Party democracy,
they advocate the end of Party discipline and the attribution of minority
rights, ... i.e. the building of fractions. This means the destruction of the
unity of purpose of the Party ... The danger of revisionism also lies in
the fact that the revisionists pretend to be developing Marxism, while
really rejecting it. (369–371)

Sectarianism is dogmatic maintenance of single theoretical statements as 124
if they alone contained the solution to all problems of political life.
Instead of studying life itself, the dogmatists use a conceptual schema and,
if the facts do not fit, they are rejected. Dogmatism is separation from
reality and if the Party does not fight against dogmatism it becomes a
sect separated from reality. (371)

Note: There follow here a few chapters which are devoted to single aspects of the
revolutionary fight and to filling out the social theses of the Third Section. The main

intent is to outline the principal possibilities of widening the action-base through *alliances*. Because of the large size of the section (125 pp.), we will limit ourselves to the main titles and a few of the most essential theses.

Chapter 14

THE POLICY OF THE UNITY OF ACTION OF THE WORKING CLASS WITH ALL DEMOCRATIC FORCES AMONG THE PEOPLE

125 In the fight for the common interests of the workers, the Communist Parties seek cooperation with all workers' organizations irrespective of their political and religious views. (377) The Communist Parties fight not only for the united front of all workers but also for the unification of wider levels of the people. The unity of the workers must serve as a basis for the unity of the broader democratic movement. (396)

126 In the democratic bloc, the role of vanguard falls to the Marxist Party of the working class, thanks to its active and selfless fight, the correctness of its political line, and its ability to always correctly judge the situation and find the solutions which are accepted by the masses. Briefly, the directive influence of the Party is the result of its own political activity and not of any pressure or command. If the Party follows correct policy and if the whole people listens not daily but hourly for its voice and authority, then the other political parties automatically recognize its leading influence and give it the decisive voice in the elaboration of the policy of the united front. (400)

Chapter 15

THE COALITION OF THE WORKING CLASS AND THE PEASANTRY UNDER CAPITALISM

127 Both by origin and by position in capitalist society, worker and peasant are blood brothers. (403) If Communists stand for an alliance of the working class and the peasantry, this is not wishful thinking. They are operating on the objective laws of social development and know that the interests of capital and the interests of the vast majority of the peasants must necessarily come into conflict. The effect of the general laws of capitalist accumulation in agriculture is the dislocation and dispersal of

the peasantry.... The vast majority of the peasants become bondsmen of capital – some go to the city and swell the ranks of the proletariat; those who stay in the village gradually become semi-proletarians. (404)

Since most of the peasants are poor in land or landless, the fight for   128
agrarian reform becomes the main goal.... Today many Communist and workers' parties unite the peasants to fight for a truly democratic agrarian reform. The main demand is: "The land belongs to those who work it". (412) At the same time Lenin showed that distribution of the land and take over of the landlords' land was not in itself enough to save the peasants from poverty, domination by the kulaks, underdevelopment, and the lower productivity of small plots. Only collective cultivation and brotherly cooperation on socialist principles can show the peasantry the way to a life of well-being. (414)

Chapter 16

THE MOVEMENT OF THE PEOPLES FOR NATIONAL LIBERATION FROM COLONIALISM[1]

The imperialists are not reconciled to the loss of their colonies. They seek   129
means of saving colonialism.... Neo-colonialism is merely the attempt to attain the usual imperialist goals through an indirect control of lands which have become formally independent. (450) The old, 'classical' colonialism did not want ... in the colonies any industries but those which produced raw materials. The spokesmen of 'neo-colonialism' are verbally for industrialization. What they desire is the establishment of light industry, mining, transport and communications – none of which is of any particular competition for foreign monopolies.... If necessary,

[1] This chapter is quite extensive (almost 40 pp.) and treats – in addition to some declarations of principle and general descriptions – of the special conditions existing in different regions of the world where an anti-colonialist fight was or is being waged. Soviet theoreticians accept the following division: "(1) countries which, after the elimination of the imperialist yoke, took the road to socialism." (China); "(2) countries which have attained political independence and follow their own foreign policy but maintain the capitalist economic system." (India, UAR, Marocco, some Latin American countries); "(3) countries which let their independence be limited by enslaving economic treaties and participation in aggressive imperialist pacts." (Pakistan); (4) the still existing colonies. (429)

the imperialists are willing to build their own factories in these lands but demand freedom to export profits and all possible guarantees against nationalization. (451)

130   American imperialism is the pacemaker of this new colonialism and is its main logistic base. (452) Some short-sighted people do not immediately see that the "anti-colonialism" of the American monopolies is only a front; they only stop playing ball with the European colonialists when they wish the latter to fail in order to replace them. And, as to American "economic aid", the lands that accept it are caught up in the militarism of American imperialism. (453)

131   Socialist countries which come out constantly against colonialism are not pursuing selfish goals. As distinguished from the USA, they do not want to take the place of any of the colonialists.... Socialist economy is incompatible with exploitation and oppression. It needs no export of capital.... The socialist states ... are not looking for markets for their surpluses, and the socialist economy does not know crises of over-production. (453) When the Soviet Union, Red China and the People's Democracies help the national aspirations of the colonial peoples, they are guided by the basic principles of socialist ideology. This is resolutely against any form of oppression and defends the equality and friendship of peoples. (453–454) The socialist states have real possibilities of helping the countries of Asia, Africa and Latin America in the creation of an independent national economy. The socialist camp is delivering – gladly and in increasing amount – tooling for industry.... The interest rates for Soviet credit are almost three times smaller than those which India is paying ... to a group of English bankers. (454–455)

Chapter 17

THE FIGHT OF THE PEOPLES OF CAPITALIST LANDS FOR THE CONSERVATION OF THEIR SOVEREIGNTY

132   Monopoly capitalism of the aggressive imperialist powers is no longer satisfied with the destruction of the sovereignty of backward and economically poor countries. It attacks the independence of economically developed and already existing sovereign bourgeois states. Although the

First World War was fought mainly for a new division of the colonies, in the Second World War German imperialism set its sights on the conquest not only of the colonies but also of the countries of the European heartland. ... After the Second World War, the monopoly capital of the USA came forward with claims to world domination. ... The reactionary circles of the USA look to limit the sovereignty ... of the independent capitalist countries. (456–457)

The workers' movement stands for the rights of nations to independence   133
and fights all forms of national oppression. (465) It is exactly the realization of the final goal of the working class – the downfall of the exploiter ... and the construction of socialism – which will give each people real freedom, independence and national pride. The most international class, the working class, is at the same time the most patriotic class. (468) The Communist Parties of the capitalist countries hold high the banner of national independence and freedom. (469) [1]

Chapter 18

THE FIGHT FOR THE DEFENCE OF DEMOCRACY IN
BOURGEOIS LANDS

The anti-democratic efforts of the monopoly bourgeoisie become stronger   134
in the period of general crisis of capitalism. The aggravation of class-war, the increasing weakness of the capitalist position and the fear before socialism, whose strength constantly rises, force the monopolies to extremes both in their domestic and foreign policies. After the First World War, fascism prevailed in some capitalist lands and openly bloody dictatorships of the most reactionary and adventurous groups of the monopoly-bourgeoisie and landowners were formed. ... The Second World War, which was carried on by the people in the name of victory over fascism, disorganized for a time the offensive of the reactionary

---

[1] The preservation of state sovereignty and the execution of an independent foreign policy are planks in the platforms of the CPs of France, Italy and other countries. The CP of England wrote in its program the demand for "execution of an independent English policy". The Progressive Workers' Party of Canada called on Canadians to "rip from the USA the national independence of Canada". The CP of Japan demanded the elimination of national oppression.... The CP of Norway said: "Norway must become a freer and more independent state!" (469)

forces in many capitalist countries.... In the post-war period came a vast attack of monopoly-capital on the democratic rights and freedoms of the peoples of capitalist lands. (476)

135 The Communists were the first victims of the reactionaries because they are the most decided opponents of capitalist slavery and the most consequential defenders of the democratic freedoms and rights of the workers. (479) The whole history of the fight of the workers in capitalist countries leads to the conclusion that democracy is indivisible. As soon as the Communist Parties were excluded, the rights and interests and, sometimes, the very existence of the other progressive organizations were endangered. (480)

136 Precisely because reduction of democracy concerned the rights of the most diverse classes and levels of the populace, there was the objective possibility of forming a broad front for democracy in capitalist lands. (481) As in other generally democratic movements, the working class is also called upon ... to play the leading role in the fight for democracy. (482) The Communist Parties of the capitalist lands are tireless in their efforts to unite the broadest popular front for the defence of democracy. (483)

Chapter 19

THE DANGER OF WAR AND THE PEOPLES' FIGHT
FOR PEACE

137 The most monstrous miscarriages of imperialism are the World Wars. Since capitalism entered its final phase, mankind has twice been thrown down into the abyss of World War ... When one takes into consideration the local wars which have been started by the imperialists in the first half of the twentieth century, then it appears that more than half this period has been spent in blood-letting. (485) An eloquent testimony to the increasingly reactionary character and aggressivity of imperialism in our day is the danger of a new World War which will be infinitely more destructive than anything mankind has suffered up to now.... The most earnest danger for peace is represented by the aggressive circles of monopoly-capital in the USA. Already on the eve of the Second World War, some representatives of American monopolies expressed their

44

desire for world domination. The financial oligarchy of Wall Street used the victory of the anti-Hitler coalition in this war for an attempt to establish the world control of the dollar. (486) In the program of their post-war expansion the monopolies of the USA set themselves vast goals: to strengthen their command position; to stifle the national liberation movements and stop the final dissolution of the colonial system by taking away from the old colonial robbers control of events; to stop the downfall of capitalism through an attempt to solve the contradictions of capitalism at the expense of the socialist camp by organizing another war. (487)

In the first years of our century Lenin wrote that the conscious portion of 138 the working class roundly condemned war as a bestial means of solving the disputed questions of mankind. Later, during the First World War, Lenin renewed his (statement) that "the socialist had always condemned war between peoples as a barbaric and bestial thing". (491) Today the Communist Parties are the most consequent defenders of peace.... They are ready to join with all organizations which oppose war and imperialism, irrespective of their motives (pacifistic, religious, moral, etc.). (492)

The Twentieth Party Congress of the Communist Party of the Soviet 139 Union also showed that there is a real possibility of avoiding war, of frustrating the plans of the war-mongers and of preserving the peace for our own and future generations.... Of course, the economic basis for war, which lies in the very nature of imperialism, is still there. Imperialism has not lost its characteristic aggressivity, lust for conquest and for war. On the contrary, it has become more militant. But, there have been recent changes in the balance of forces in the world which make it possible to restate the question on the possibility of a successful fight for peace. (496)

An important historical peculiarity of the present – which creates 140 extraordinarily good conditions for the preservation of peace – is the existence of the socialist camp which follows a consequently peace-loving policy. (497) Reactionary propaganda is always talking ... about the danger of "world-Communism" which supposedly threatens the freedom of the Western world.... Yet ever wider masses throughout the world are beginning to see that the Communist Parties and Communist countries have no reason to wish a war and to plan military attacks on other countries. (498)

141   The official doctrine of Soviet foreign policy is the Leninist principle of the peaceful coexistence of states, irrespective of the differences in their social and governmental structures. (499)

Chapter 20

ON THE DIFFERENT FORMS OF THE TRANSITION
TO SOCIALIST REVOLUTION

142   The merciless exploitation of the workers, plundering of the peasantry and urban middle classes by the monopolies, the attacks on democracy and the danger of fascism, the national oppression and the danger of a new and destructive war – all of this has, ultimately, one source, i.e. capitalism. In order to free the workers from class-oppression, to put a definitive end to war, to ensure real democracy, freedom and independence for the people, an end must be made of capitalism and the socialist revolution must be accomplished. In the wide sense, *socialist revolution* means the totality of the political and economic transformations which lead to the complete liquidation of capitalism and to the construction of socialism. It begins with the political transformation, i.e. breaking the power of the capitalists and setting up the power of the workers. This political transformation is also called in Marxist theory the proletarian revolution. It is clear that the road to such a transformation is not perfectly smooth so that one can succeed without great efforts and political know-how. The passage of the masses of millions – of whole classes and social levels – to the decisive battle for power is a complicated and many-faceted process. (502)

143   No matter how wide and varied the social forces involved in the downfall of capitalism might be, the decisive role in the socialist revolution is played by the working class. It is the main attacking force ... Even in less developed capitalist lands where the working class is a minority, it is best able – as the most organized and conscious social class – to unite, under the direction of its Marxist-Leninist vanguard, all the working levels of the population for the fight for socialism. *A fortiori* is this the case in lands with developed capitalism. (502–503)

144   The fight of the revolutionary workers' Party for the socialist revolution corresponds to the basic trend of social progress. The very development

46

of contemporary capitalism drags the workers in this direction. (503) The proletarian revolution is a direct and open collision of two main protagonists: the working class and the bourgeoisie. However, the social revolution never has the character of a bilateral fight ... The contradictions between the working class and the bourgeoisie can be complicated by those between the peasantry and landlords, landlords and bourgeoisie, large and small bourgeoisie, monopolies and the other parts of the populace. (504)

Different sorts of movements of the oppressed and discontented masses   145 can lead to proletarian revolution, if only the conscious vanguard of the working class understands how to lead these movements into the revolutionary path. The principal types of contemporary democratic movements which are against monopoly-capital and against imperialism were mentioned in the previous chapters [1]: the fight of the peasant masses against the remains of feudalism, which are preserved by imperialism, and their anti-monopoly movement; the national-liberation movement of the peoples of colonial and dependent lands, and the patriotic fight for the preservation of independence; the fight for the defence of democracy, the peoples' move for world peace, the humanistic movement of the intelligentsia and their defence of culture. Also of democratic character are the movements for the nationalization of the property of capitalistic monopolies, ... for increasing the rights of women and children ... These movements are called democratic or general-democratic because they fight for democratic aims rather than for socialist goals. (506)

It is not impossible that under certain conditions the democratic move-   146 ments against the policies of the imperialist bourgeoisie can turn into democratic revolutions. These revolutions would be anti-monopolistic since they aim at the destruction of the bigger monopolies. Their driving force would be the working class, the peasantry, the urban middle classes and the democratic intelligentsia ... As historical experience has shown, democratic revolutions in the era of imperialism do not restrict themselves to the accomplishment of purely democratic tasks, but rather show a tendency to develop further – to a higher level. (509) The most likely development of such a revolution is its transformation into a socialist revolution. (514)

[1] Chapters 15 through 19, the content of which we only sketched.

147 Of decisive significance for the transformation of popular, democratic revolutions into socialist revolutions is the presence of strong Marxist-Leninist Parties which have strong support in all parts of the population, and the elastic and clever politics of these parties. (515)

148 The democratic, anti-monopolistic revolution is a possible but not unavoidable step in the fight for socialism in present-day capitalist lands. It is possible that the general-democratic movements not lead to such revolutions ... and that the socialist transformation come directly without the general-democratic step. (515)

THE RIPENING OF THE CONDITIONS FOR THE PROLETARIAN REVOLUTION

149 The socialist revolution is a vast and complicated affair involving participation of millions of men and with different class-forces, parties and organizations conflicting and working on one another. It is clear that even when the revolution is fully ripe, when the basic class-oppositions of capitalist society are aggravated to the highest, it cannot succeed in a willy-nilly, arbitrarily chosen moment and situation. Very definite conditions are necessary in order that the proletarian revolution succeed and that the power fall into the hands of the workers. (517–518) Up to now, it has been the case in the development of history that the revolutionary overthrow of capitalism and the falling away of countries from the capitalist system have always been tied up with a World War ... It does not, however, follow that future revolutionary victories over capitalism must have war as a prerequisite. Even though world wars without revolution are unthinkable, revolutions are perfectly possible without war. (519)

150 Marxism-Leninism teaches that the proletarian revolution is the result of an extreme aggravation of social and political contradictions. Meanwhile, such an aggravation is in our era ... a permanent state in most capitalist countries. In order that the internal contradictions of capitalism break out violently, one need not wait for war or any other external stimulus. Because of the high level of consciousness and organization achieved by the revolutionary workers' movement in our time and the presence of favorable international conditions, the revolutionary explosion

can also be the result of those processes going on in the economic and political life of the capitalist countries. (520)

Every revolution which deserves the name is the action of broad popular 151 masses which have risen up to selfless fight with full determination to change the social order and their conditions of existence. But, when it is question of whole classes and peoples, it would be naive to think that they could be set in motion on someone's whim. Peoples and classes rise up to fight because of motives which are deep in their objective living conditions. Leninism has elaborated general criteria for deciding if the conditions are ripe for revolution and if the objective situation is favorable to the masses' fight for power. In the language of politics such a favorable state of affairs is called a revolutionary situation. (520)

A *revolutionary situation* comes to be when the policies of the ruling classes 152 have become bankrupt and have led them into a blind alley, when the popular masses are completely dissatisfied and confusion reigns in the upper classes . . . Among the *objective* factors which aid the situation it is, as a rule, the economic factors which are decisive, i.e. an essential aggravation of the want and misery of the oppressed classes. Extraordinary increase of exploitation, massive unemployment, quickly rising taxes, crisis in the economy, which robs the masses of their hope in tomorrow and the future – all of this doubtlessly renders probable the outbreak of the revolutionary activities of the masses. But Marxists never treat the material causes as the sole factors which revolutionize the consciousness and will of the working masses. . . . Elements of a revolutionary explosion are piled up in capitalist lands by such things as increased danger of military adventures and the rebirth of fascism. The danger of falling with one's country into an atomic catastrophe can very quickly consolidate the masses to open attack on the power of the political adventurers . . . Unbridled political reaction can also lead to ripening of a revolutionary situation. The same role can be played by such things as the danger of occupation of one's land by foreign troops. (521–522)

However, revolution – as Lenin pointed out – does not result from every 153 revolutionary situation; it only comes when to the necessary objective conditions are added the *subjective* ones. An important role is played by the ability and preparedness of the revolutionary classes to decided action which is strong enough to break or totter the existing power which never – even in periods of crisis – falls by itself if one does not bring it down. It is precisely in the periods of revolutionary crisis that the political maturity and ability to fight of the Parties of the working class are put to the test. (522) Without the leadership of the Party, the revolution is impossible . . . (523)

THE PASSING OF POWER INTO THE HANDS OF THE WORKING CLASS

154   The central question of every revolution is the question of power. . . . The task of the proletarian revolution is to take power from the reactionary bourgeoisie and its political representatives and to give it to the working class and its allies. This revolution takes political power from the exploiter-classes and destroys the bases of their economic power. It opens a new historical period, the period of the transition from capitalism to socialism. (523)

155   Before every working class Party – when it is leading the masses along the road of the proletarian revolution – arises the question as to the character – peaceful or non-peaceful – which the transition will have. This depends, first of all, on the objective conditions: the situation of the country in question, the level of development of the class-war, the intensity and strength of the resistance of the ruling classes, and also the international situation. Therein it must be remembered that the choice of weapons in each revolution does not depend on one side. In the socialist revolution, it does not depend on the working class alone but also on the bourgeoisie and its representatives who are defending the crumbling walls of the exploiter-order. (524)

156   The working class is not determined to solve all social problems by force. Lenin always stressed that "the working class would prefer, of course, to take power peacefully". . . . History teaches that the ruling classes do not give up their power and leave the historical scene of their own will. Strengthened by the governmental apparatus, they crush with force even the smallest revolutionary moves and every attempt to take away their class-privileges. Therefore, the traditional form of political transformation is the armed revolt of the revolutionary classes against the old ruling classes. (524)

50

The enemies of socialism have been trying for years to distort the relation-   157
ship between Marxism-Leninism and armed uprising and its place in
socialist revolution. They tried and try to represent the Communists as
conspirators and plotters who, behind the backs of the masses, try to take
the power. There is not the slightest truth in such contentions. . . .
Lenin. . . always conceived the revolt as a vast action of the working
masses, lead by the conscious portion of the working class. Five months
before the October Revolution, in May 1917, Lenin said: "A 'seizure of
power' is not what we want since all revolutionary experience shows that
power is durable only if based on the majority of the population". (525)

There are great advantages to the peaceful transition to socialism. It   158
allows the basic changing of social life with a minimum of victims among
the workers, with minimal destruction of the forces of production of
society, and with least disruption of the process of production. . . .
Peaceful seizure of power best corresponds to the whole world-outlook
of the working class. Its great humanistic ideals exclude the use of force
for the sake of force and even more because the power of historical truth –
of which the working class is the bearer – is so great that it is fully able to
count on the support of the vast majority of the population. The question,
therefore, is not if the Marxists and revolutionary workers wish the
peaceful revolution, but if the objective conditions for it are present. (526)
The real Marxist is marked by elasticity in the application of the various
forms of revolution. (527)

Where the military-police force of the reactionary bourgeoisie is powerful,   159
the working class meets bitter opposition. It is not in doubt that in a series
of capitalist countries the bourgeois dictatorship will only be overthrown
through armed class-war. . . . It would be a great error not to reckon with
this eventuality and to prepare for the bitter resistance of reaction.
(529)

A possible form of peaceful transition to socialism is the winning of   160
power by the working class through obtaining a parliamentary majority.
(529) The parliamentary path to socialism has a series of advantages for
the working class. The forming of the new power by an institution which
is as traditional in many lands as is the parliament would provide the
necessary authority and facilitate the socialist transformations to follow.

Any opposition to socialist transformations would be, in such a case, both *de facto* and *de jure* illegal and against the popular will as expressed by the parliament. (530) The parliamentary fight guarantees the transition to socialism only when it is based on the revolutionary mass-movement of the working class and the broader levels of the population. (531)

161   In the Marxist-Leninist theory of socialist revolution the question on the relationship between the general laws of revolution and national peculiarities has an important place.... The revisionists are against the recognition of the general laws of revolution and over-emphasize the national peculiarities.... The dogmatists, on the other hand, ignore the necessity of taking the national peculiarities into account.... Marxism-Leninism maintains that – irrespective of the concrete conditions and national traditions – the revolution has certain important, general traits and laws. I.e., the dissolution of capitalism by socialism is in all lands fundamentally the same process. It begins with two fundamental transformations: (1) The exploiting classes are dragged from political power and the rule of the workers led by the working class – the dictatorship of the proletariat – is installed; (2) the property of the capitalists and landowners is seized and social ownership of the main means of production is established. These two transformations can ... take place in different ways. But, in all cases where the working class carries out the transition to socialism, these changes must take place. Without them there is no socialism. (523–533)

DOCTRINE ON SOCIALISM AND COMMUNISM

Chapter 21

THE DICTATORSHIP OF THE PROLETARIAT AND PROLETARIAN DEMOCRACY

The socialist transformation brings to power the workers under the leadership of the working class.... This transformation begins the period of transition from capitalism to socialism.... As the classics of Marxism-Leninism taught, the force which turns this transformation into reality can only be the revolutionary dictatorship of the proletariat. (535).   162

THE NECESSITY OF THE DICTATORSHIP OF THE PROLETARIAT

All revolutions have to overcome the resistance of the reactionary classes.... The socialist revolution is such a thorough-going social transformation – it destroys all exploitation of man by man – that it must overcome an especially strong resistance.... As long as the period of transition is not completed, said Lenin, "the exploiters inevitably hope for restoration and this hope leads to attempts at restoration". (536).   163

The hopes of the reactionary bourgeoisie for a restoration are nourished by the fact that, although they have lost political power, they are still reasonably strong. In the beginning, they still have a series of advantages over the victorious working class.[1] (537).   164

---

[1] The bourgeoisie can count on the help of international capital.... Further, as long as the dethroned exploiting classes have not lost all ownership of the means of production, they still have certain positions in the economy. They use these for sabotage and disorganization of the economy. Having lost political power, the bourgeoisie seeks economic revenge, creating enormous difficulties for the new power.... In the first period after the revolution, (they) have better education, experience in the organization of production and such other advantages as relations with the technocracy and military specialists. For quite a while, the bourgeoisie is able to ideologically and politically influence the masses. This influence is the more nefarious in that the workers cannot immediately free themselves from the blows of century-long exploitation. In addition, imperialism leaves behind it a mass of uprooted and criminal elements – above all, from the ruined petty bourgeoisie. These supply mercenaries for the counterrevolution. (537–538)

165 There is no socialist land where the reactionary classes did not offer resistance to revolutionary change. The character of this resistance differed according to the various class-forces in presence.... In order to insure the victory of the revolution and to break the resistance of the ousted classes, it was everywhere necessary to exercise a strong and decisive power and, when necessary, not to shy away from the use of force. (538)

166 Following its noble and humane ideals, the working class tried to pick the appropriate means. "The end justifies the means" is the solution of the Jesuits, not of Communists. Communists do their best to get along without the use of force both during the fight for power and during the construction of socialism. If the working class must, nevertheless, use force, this is due to the resistance of the ousted classes and, therefore, is the fault not of the new socialist society but of the old capitalist one. (539)

167 Those who believe that the dictatorship of the proletariat and the use of force against the violent is contrary to humanism are in error. The contrary is the case. The more firm the new power is, less founded will be the hopes of the reactionaries for a restoration and less necessary will be the recourse to force. (539)

168 Bourgeois propaganda seeks to represent political repression exclusively as terror, reprisals and direct limitations of democratic rights. Such extreme measures are only used against active resistance on the part of the bourgeoisie. If the ousted classes take up arms, they meet the firm action of workers' power.... But, in other cases, peaceable means can be used, leading to gradual elimination of the causes of the existence of the exploiting classes: nationalization of capitalist property, attracting to work and educating the loyally inspired portion of the bourgeoisie, etc. However, under no circumstances can the dictatorship of the proletariat be based on compromise and lawlessness. On the contrary, it creates a strict, revolutionary legality in the land by demanding strict adherance to the law both by the citizens and the officials of the new power. (539–540)

169 The question on the dictatorship of the proletariat is the center of the

ideological differences of opinion between the Marxist-Leninists and the reformists. The doctrine on the proletarian dictatorship as the only means of putting an end to the horror and degradation of the exploiter-society was and is the touchstone of the rectitude and sincerity of the socialist desires of the workers' parties and their leaders. (541)...
Historical experience with the proletarian revolution in a series of Western countries (France, Germany, Hungary, Finland) has shown that the exploiting classes resort to the most extreme measures in order to maintain their power. If the working class underestimates this and takes no measures to hamstring the bourgeoisie, it will have a high price to pay. (543)

A NEW TYPE OF DEMOCRACY

With the victory of the working class, the era of rule by a privileged   170
minority comes to an end and the era of real popular rule begins. Workers, peasants, artisans and the working intelligentsia, who were kept from political life for centuries, now begin to rule the state as their own. This characterizes proletarian democracy as a new type of democracy, higher than bourgeois democracy. (544) History has verified that dictatorship and democracy can be excellently combined. The state, which is dictatorship for some classes can, at the same time, be democracy for other classes.... The dictatorship of the working class is essentially a most deeply democratic power since it is the rule of the majority over the minority while the dictatorship of the bourgeoisie is the rule of the minority over the majority. (545–546) Bourgeois scholars and publicists often present the following argument. Democracy, they say, necessarily requires the conflict of parties, the existence of opposition in parliament, etc. Having listed these formal characteristics of bourgeois democracy and finding that one or another is lacking in the socialist countries, they triumphantly announce that the proletarian dictatorship is an undemocratic system. Marxists judge otherwise the democratic character of a political system. One must ask: what interests does state power protect, who it serves, what policy does it maintain, etc. From this uniquely scientific point of view, one finds in the bourgeois states no real popular rule.... Only proletarian democracy offers real popular rule since it serves the interests of the workers, i.e. of the majority of society. (546)

171   While proletarian democracy offers democratic rights as never before to the worker, it cannot do the same for the ousted reactionary forces of the bourgeoisie, etc., who are fighting for restoration of capitalism. This is the limit of proletarian democracy. Socialist revolution would suffer the greatest harm if the organizations of the great capitalists were guaranteed political freedom. (547)

172   Proletarian democracy means the transition from the formal democracy of the bourgeois republic to factual participation of the working masses in the administration.... Universal suffrage is the highest that bourgeois democracy can offer. The masses have the right to vote but, in fact, are kept away as before from participation in government. The socialist revolution, opens to broad sections of the popular masses the possibility of taking daily, practical part in the affairs of the state both directly through the governmental institutions and indirectly through the social organizations, the numerous sections, commissions and councils accredited to the state administration. Another essential characteristic of proletarian democracy is the spread of democratic administration not only to politics but also to the direction of the economy and of culture. (549)

THE MARXIST-LENINIST PARTY DURING THE DICTATORSHIP OF THE PROLETARIAT

173   The acquisition of power by the working class completely changes the situation of its militant vanguard, the Marxist-Leninist Party.... The experience of the socialist countries shows that the importance of the Marxist Party as leader of the working class and all workers after the revolution is not only not reduced but incomparably increased. It is now responsible for all that happens in society; for the policies of the government of the dictatorship of the proletariat, for the development of the forces of production, for culture, for the growth of the well-being of the people. The revolutionary changes to be accomplished by the power of the working class are so complex and the forces which oppose the construction of the new society are so great that success can be had only through complete unity of will of the proletariat and profound under-

standing of the laws of social development – in a word, through a clear action program. The working class receives all of this from its vanguard which is its most conscious and firmly decided section and which is capable of consequently expressing the interests of the proletariat and of all workers. (551–552)

In the period of the fight for power, the appearance of many workers' 174 parties is possible. If, however, there is no unity of action among them, the fight of the working class is singularly impeded. After the victory of the working class it is necessary, as a rule to have a single Marxist-Leninist Party in order to assure the firmness of the new power and to guarantee unity of will in the leadership of society. (552)

How does the party realize its directive role during the dictatorship of the 175 proletariat? It works through the governmental administration and social mass-organizations, the efforts of which it concentrates on single goals. Even though it directs all governmental and social organizations, it does not replace them. The directorial power of the Party can be compared to that of the conductor of an orchestra who produces harmony but does not try to play each musician's part. The Party guarantees the realization of its policies by working through its members who, in turn, work in the administration and in social organizations. (553)

The unanimity of the Party is even more important during the dictator- 176 ship of the proletariat. Since class-war does not cease but takes on more complicated forms, the Party is under constant pressure not only from the remains of the capitalist classes who oppose the construction of socialism but also from the deviations of weaker elements among the workers. Since the Party is the leader and unifying force of the dictator-ship of the proletariat, destruction of its unity can ... lead to burying the dictatorship. (554–555)

The bourgeois state is by nature bureaucratic. Under capitalism, bureau- 177 cratism is an administrative system wherein power is held by a bureau-cracy which is alienated from the people, not controlled by the people and subservient to the needs of the exploiter-class. It is clear that bureau-cratism is no essential trait of the state of the working class since this state is created by the people, serves the people and is controlled by the people. Therefore, long after its victory the working class must lead a fight against bureaucratism and especially against its formalism, mercilessness, alienation from the people, and proneness to routine. Bureaucratic deformations under the dictatorship of the proletariat are leftovers of the capitalist system. . . . The internal democracy of the dictatorship of the proletariat provides the necessary conditions for the successful overcoming of bureaucratic tendencies through ever-wider participation of the masses in the administration and through use of various forms of control from below. (556–557)

DIVERSE FORMS OF THE DICTATORSHIP OF THE PROLETARIAT

178   The forms taken by the dictatorship of the proletariat depend on the inter-relation of class-forces in the revolution and on the directness of their collision. If the ruling classes offer strong resistance and the revolution takes on a violent character, the working class is forced to level all the old political institutions on which the bourgeoisie is dependent. On the contrary, if in the course of the revolution there is a great advantage in favor of the anti-reactionary forces so that power can come to the working class by peaceful means, then it is possible to use some of the old instruments of power, e.g., the parliament which one can reconstruct in the interests of socialist construction. (557–558)

179   *Soviet power.* The first government of the dictatorship of the proletariat was established in Russia in the form of soviets of workers, soldiers and peasants. . . . What was the specific character of the soviets? They were openly class-organizations since they guaranteed the vote and office-holding only for the workers, peasants and those working intelligentsia who cooperated. . . . The development of the class-war in the country led to the formation of a one party-system for the political leadership of the soviets. (558–559)

180   *Popular democracy.* The development of the international liberation movement created another form of worker's rule, the people's democracies. After the Second World War, this form was established in a series of countries of Middle and South-East Europe and of Asia. (560) . . . In the course of the liberation war against fascism . . . a common front of anti-

58

fascist, democratic forces was formed. (560) The broader social base of the revolution demanded a new type of governmental power of the working class. In this way the popular democracy developed as a new form of popular rule, filling the functions of the dictatorship of the proletariat.... As distinct from Soviet power, the people's democracy did not take up the functions of the dictatorship of the proletariat immediately. In some countries, the Communist and Workers' Parties did not immediately have a firm majority in parliament and in the coalition regimes.... This state is a transitional type and its further fate depends on the relationship of class-forces within the whole democratic bloc and on the outcome of the class-war between the workers and bourgeois elements of the right. (561)

The broad coalition of class-forces on which the people's democracy is   181
based permits a wide enjoyment of political democracy. Only an insignificant number of peons of the fascist occupation and traitors to the people are subjected to limitations of political rights. (562)

Other possible forms. Soviet power and the popular democracy confirm   182
that the basic traits of the working-class state are everywhere the same. However history repeats itself in basic lines though not in details; the transition of other peoples to socialism can doubtlessly produce other forms of working-class power. In lands with century-long parliamentary traditions, the parliamentary republic could become a form of the dictatorship of the working class or a corresponding form of popular power. (564–565) Undoubtedly, the liberation movements in the countries of Asia, South America, Africa and the Near East ... will give birth to new forms of political power of the workers. (566)

However, regardless of the form of transition of one country or another   183
from capitalism to socialism, there are certain basic laws. The most important of these are – as declared by a consultation of representatives of Communist and Workers' Parties: the directorial role of the working class and its Marxist-Leninist Party in the accomplishment of the proletarian revolution and the establishment of the dictatorship of the proletariat; the coalition of the working class with the main body of peasants and with the other levels of workers; the protection of the achievements of socialism against the attacks of external and internal enemies. (566)

Chapter 22

THE MAIN ECONOMIC TASKS DURING THE PERIOD OF TRANSITION FROM CAPITALISM TO SOCIALISM

184   The working class takes power in order to use political rule for the destruction of capitalism and the construction of socialism. This requires, above all, a fundamental transformation of the economy. (567) Economically speaking, the main task in the transitional period is the socialization of the means of production, the rapid development of the socialist sector and the organization of new, socialist relations of production on this base. (568)

SOCIALIST NATIONALIZATION

185   The first act in the transformation of the economy is the nationalization of capitalist heavy industry. (568) Socialist nationalization is a universally necessary task of the socialist revolution, no matter where it takes place.... In all countries where there are large land-holdings ... their confiscation is a primordial task of the working class. (571)

186   Characteristic of the economic situation of the transition period is multiformity.... And a very important economic and political task of the Party and the workers' state is the overcoming of this multiformity. Normally, three economic forms are characteristic of the first period after the victory of the revolution: socialism, small industry and private capitalism. The corresponding classes are: the working class, the peasantry and the ousted but not eliminated bourgeoisie. (574–575) But the elimination of multiformity is a very complicated affair, and one which cannot be carried out by a cavalry charge, through decree or command. (567)

COOPERATIVES

187   The most difficult economic task of the transition period is the socialization of the splintered small industry.... The main consideration is that the peasantry is the main ally of the working class and cannot be dispossessed; attention must rather be paid to the establishment of strong economic ties. (577) Sooner or later, it is necessary to help the mass of the peasantry to gradually turn from small, individual production to large,

machine-equipped agriculture.... Similarly, the policies of the dictatorship of the proletariat concerning the richer peasants must sooner or later turn from limiting measures to those designed to eliminate them as a class. The sole path to the creation of socialized large-scale production in agriculture is the gradual transformation of the property of small peasants into cooperative property.... The socialist way of reorganizing agriculture is the voluntary formation of peasant cooperatives. (580–581) The cooperative is the most accessible, understandable and advantageous form of economic community for the peasant.... This does not mean that the formation of agricultural cooperatives is an automatic thing. No, it requires the constant and all-round support of the Party and government – financial and organizational support. Also necessary is political help for the working peasantry since their transition to collectivization is, as a rule, accompanied by class-war which can for a time be quite violent. It happens that in the course of forming the agricultural cooperatives the fate of the last exploiting class – the kulaks – is sealed.... The prerequisites for the destruction of the kulaks as a class are established.[1] (582–583)

As experience has shown, the Communist Parties often encounter in the course of full collectivization the danger of leftist extremism, i.e. attempts to carry out this task without regard for the degree of preparation of the peasants, to be hasty where it is not necessary and not to convince the men involved. Against these methods which forget the Leninist principle of freedom of choice, the Communist Parties have to fight not only in the beginning stages of the massive formation of cooperatives but also thenceforward. However, a greater danger is presented by rightist deviations which either put off the formation of cooperatives to a distant future or slow their execution to a snail's pace... (584–585)   188

The main goal of the dictatorship of the proletariat is the defeat of private property above all in public economic competition. The proletarian state does not fear such competition. It has in its hands a powerful industry and the instruments for directing the economy. The advantages of highly organized and concentrated socialist heavy industry bring it,   189

---

[1] Naturally this does not mean the physical annihilation of the representatives of this class but the elimination of the social and economic conditions which make it possible for the village bourgeoisie to exploit the poor peasants and agricultural workers. (583)

sooner or later, economic victory over private capital in all economic domains. The field of activity of private capital is limited and the only escape is economic capitulation. ... As practice has shown, different forms of government-capitalism ... play an important role. ... Under the dictatorship of the proletariat, this is a capitalism which is under the control of the workers' state; it is a form of use of private capital for the construction of socialism. ... The industrialists who loyally work with the state often draw advantages from the creation of mixed, private-governmental firms and contracts. ... As regards the future, experience shows that the proletarian state can make the transition of the loyal capitalist to an active working life as light and painless as possible. Materially, this transition is buffered by the fact that the capitalist receives for a while compensation for the seized property; morally, by the fact that the state values his knowledge and ability and offers him corresponding tasks in the factories, and political rights in the context of proletarian democracy. (586–588)

SOCIALIST INDUSTRIALIZATION

190 The material conditions for socialism are already present, at least partially, in the womb of capitalism. Which does not mean that, after the revolution, the workers' power will face no new tasks in this domain. (588) The tasks which present themselves in the creation of the material-technical base of socialism are different in different countries. In agricultural countries, it is the rapid development of industry. In countries which already had under capitalism a highly developed level of production, it is an essential reorganization of the industrial structure, the construction of new commercial relations and the overcoming of past disproportions. (591)

191 The socialists of the right cry out that the question of the seizure of power should not even be posed until the whole economy has reached the high level which is characteristic of developed government-monopoly capitalism. ... The Russian working class paid no attention to these pedants. It first took power and then began to conquer economic and cultural backwardness and to form technicians for the economy. ... Economic and technological backwardness was not, therefore, an unconquerable obstacle in the construction of socialism. Of course, the working class

faced grandiose and most difficult tasks: the creation of the material-technical base of socialism, the development of all branches of industry especially of the fabrication of the means of production. These tasks are faced by all lands which take the road to socialism but especially by those who previously had no sufficiently developed industrial base. In other words, they are faced by the necessity for a socialist industrialization. (589)

The means for the socialist industrialization can only come from internal 192 resources which are fabricated by the work of the worker, peasant and intelligentsia. Of course, this will require some victims and create some difficulties – especially in the first stage of socialist industrialization. (590)

THE RESULTS OF THE PERIOD OF TRANSITION

The main result of the period of transition is the victory of the socialist 193 mode of production. The socialist economic form ... from the leading to the ruling finally becomes the sole one in the economy. Small production of the peasants and artisans is changed into a socialist system through the formation of cooperatives. The capitalist economic form completely disappears as a result of the limitations and eliminations of capitalist elements in the economy...(592) In the transition period are formed new, socialist relations of distribution. With the elimination of the parasitic classes, the national income comes fully into the possession of the workers. ... As a result of the fulfilment of the economic tasks of the transition period, unemployment – the scourge of the working class under capitalism – is eliminated even before the full victory of socialist work-relations. Forever, also, disappear the causes of poverty in the village. The right to work is realized for the first time and guaranteed by the planned development of the socialist economy. (593)

Chapter 23

THE BASIC TRAITS OF THE SOCIALIST MODE
OF PRODUCTION

The transition from capitalism to socialism ends with the firm establish- 194 ment of social ownership in all branches of the national economy.

Socialism now develops on the basis of mechanized heavy industry and collective, mechanized agriculture. Society itself, the workers have the possibility to plan and regulate the process of production at the national-economic level. Under capitalism a more or less planned organization of production is possible only within one enterprise or monopoly. But, even this planning is negated by the anarchy which reigns throughout the economy. Socialism includes the possibility of planned direction of the mechanism of social production in its entirety. (595)

195 A new era begins in the history of mankind, the era of planned economy. The extent of social production, its structure, the division of work and of the means of production among the branches of the economy, prices, wages – all of this is no longer spontaneous. Society itself plans in order to ever more fully satisfy the needs of its members. However, this does not mean that the objective laws of the economy cease to work. On the contrary, in order that conscious activity in the direction of the economy be most effective, socialist society must be directed by the objective laws of its development and organize its economy in accord with these laws. (595)

SOCIAL PROPERTY AND ITS FORMS

196 Marx opined that the mode and main elements of the production process form a whole – work and means of production – which forms the base of every social order. Under socialism these elements are united so that the producers own the work-instruments which they use. This completely excludes the transformation of the means of production into means of exploitation of one part of the society. As co-owners of social property and participants in the process of social production, all men are equal and found their relations on the basis of comradely cooperation and mutual help. (596)

197 Social property ... exists in two forms: general property of the people (governmental) and cooperative-collective. (596) General property of the people is in socialism property of the government since society ... is represented at this stage by the state. ... When one says that under socialism men consciously direct their social development, one means that this is done by the Party and the state which exercise the functions of leaders and organizers of the socialist economy. (597)

64

In addition to state property, Marxist-Leninists also recognize under 198
socialism cooperative or group-property as a fully justified form and
develop and perfect it in every way.... Cooperative property originates
historically under socialism as the result of the special path taken by the
peasantry and other population levels... to reach new, collective
economic forms. That collective property which comes to be through
cooperatives of small producers is the cooperative-collective form of
socialist property. It is the group property of the agricultural artel [1]
(kolhoz), of the artisanal cooperatives and of other cooperative ventures.
(599–600)

In comparison to governmental, general popular property, cooperative 199
property is a less ripe form of socialist property. The means of production
and the product do not belong to the whole society but to the collective in
question.... The cooperative form ... passes through a series of developmental stages, from lower to higher.... Thus, ... the cooperative
forms come nearer and nearer to the popular, governmental enterprises.
(600–601)

THE MAIN OBJECT OF SOCIALIST PRODUCTION

The object of capitalist production is gain or profit.... The transforma- 200
tion of the means of production into social property basically changes the
motives and goals of production. Under socialism the means of production belong to the workers, i.e. to society, and it is clear that the workers
cannot exploit themselves.... The entirety of the social product which is
yearly produced in the socialist economy belongs to those who own the
means of production, to society, to the workers taken as a productive
collectivity of the whole people. (601)

Under socialism the task of society is the ever fuller satisfaction of the 201
constantly growing material and cultural needs of all its members. The
ever richer satisfaction of needs as the goal of socialist production is a
necessary, law-bound occurrence.... In Soviet economic writings this
law is called "the basic economic law of socialism" and is formulated as
follows: the uninterrupted expansion and perfection of production on the

[1] The artel is a cooperative grouping of producers, which existed even before the
revolution.

65

basis of progressive technology with the goal of the most perfect satisfaction of the constantly growing needs and all-round development of all members of society. (602)

202   History has run so that the first socialist lands to enter into economic competition with capitalism were those which were economically backward in the past. In order to win in this competition, they had to have a high rate of growth of production, to exert great efforts and to overcome numerous difficulties – all bound up with their previous backwardness. A high growth rate is reached only when all branches of production are provided with the newest equipment and this demands a high rate of accumulation, i.e. the availability of a large portion of the national income for the expansion of production. The extent of consumer investments has been limited even up to now by the fact that the socialist countries have to spend considerable amounts for defence. (603)

THE PLANNED DEVELOPMENT OF THE NATIONAL ECONOMY

203   Under socialism the national economy is an organic whole, directed by a single will. Under these conditions, the first prerequisite of the economy is the assurance of harmony, the maximal and mutual agreement of all sections of the social mechanism of production in the country. This prerequisite is expressed in the law of the proportional development of the national economy. What is the essence of this law? Above all, that for a normal functioning of the socialist economy certain mutual relations and proportions are necessary between its different sections. And, further, that the establishment and maintenance of such proportions under socialism is to be planned, i.e. to be the result of preconceived measures of the socialist state and its planning institutions. (603–604) An overall proportion between the development of heavy and light industry, between the production of raw materials and finished products must be controlled. The pledge of progress in all branches of the economy is the high-priority development of heavy industry. (605)

204   There is no eternally established and unchangeable relationship between production and consumption and between consumption and accumulation. Consumption grows on the basis of the increase in labor productivity. With the appearance of new tasks in socialist construction and with

changes in the international situation, the previous tempo of accumulation can prove to be too small or too large. The socialist planning system serves to correctly estimate changes underway, to introduce – when necessary – the required adjustments of the economic plan, to anticipate disproportions in the economy or, in any case, to quickly correct them when they do occur.[1] (606–607)

WORK UNDER SOCIALISM

The division of society into a working majority and a leisured minority   205
which lives through exploitation is impossible under socialism since work becomes the sole source of income. When all basic means of production are concentrated in the hands of the socialist state and the production-cooperatives, each man's work loses its private character and becomes social in nature. This means that the work of each man serves the fulfilment of a determined portion of the economic plan.... The directly social character of work ... fosters the development of new drives in the workers. In addition to material interests, moral drives to work develop. Thereby, work changes from a pure means in life to a matter of pride.... In place of the old work-discipline based on force is developed a new, conscious one, based on the understanding which every worker has of his duty toward society and his own interest in work. The new relation to work and solicitude of the workers for the development of social production comes to light in *socialist competition*. (615)

The principle of distribution. The material and cultural goods are distri-   206
buted quantitatively and qualitatively under socialism according to the work which each worker supplies in social production. Whence the necessity of keeping strict accounts of the amount of work and the level of consumption. He who works more and better, is better payed by the socialist society for his work.... The socialist principle "from each according to his abilities, to each according to his accomplishment" demands amelioration of the qualifications of the worker and their constant fight to increase the productivity of work. Egalitarianism in the remuneration of work is contradictory to the interests of socialism. (618)

[1] The next section is devoted to the details of economic planning, especially to the place of calculation of value and of production of goods. (609–614)

WIDENED SOCIALIST REPRODUCTION

207   The national income of socialist society is divided into a consumer fund and an accumulation fund. In the U.S.S.R. some 75% of the national income goes into the consumer fund. (622) In order to constantly increase the production of the national economy, the relationship between section I and II [1] must be so arranged that the first has a higher rate of growth. . . . The high-priority growth in the production of means of production guarantees the increase of technical equipment in all branches of the national economy and, consequently, an increase of the productivity of work. (619–620)

208   The bourgeois economists and the reformists spread the belief that all efforts in socialist lands are directed only toward the development of heavy industry and war-production, and not toward the production of consumer goods. But the rapid increase of consumption of the most important goods in the socialist countries refutes this calumny of socialism. Historical experience has proved that the high-priority growth in the production of the means of production in socialist countries is not an end in itself but a means necessary for the realization of the main task of socialist production, i.e. the elevation of the well-being of the people. (23)

Chapter 24

THE SOCIAL-POLITICAL AND CULTURAL PHAENOTYPE OF SOCIALIST SOCIETY

209   The transformation of the means of production into social property causes the fundamental reconstruction of all social relations, viz. the political superstructure, the ideology, culture, the way of life, the mores and habits. (624)

THE STRUCTURE OF SOCIALIST SOCIETY

210   As a result of the economic and social changes in the transition period, a new class-structure forms in society. The exploiting classes are fully

---

[1] Section I is the production of the means of production; Section II is the production of consumer goods.

eliminated, i.e. the classes of capitalists, landowners and rich peasants. Society has become a society of workers, i.e. workers, peasants and intelligentsia. Their situation is radically different. This is especially true of the *working class*. From a class which was robbed of the means of production, it has become – along with the whole people – the owners thereof; from an exploited class, it has become the leading class of society. . . . It is also the most important bearer of Communist consciousness. In the world of the worker there are incomparably fewer remnants of the owner-psychology which still marks a part of the peasantry, and of the individualism still present in some representatives of the intelligentsia. The traditions of socialist collaboration and collective solidarity are here deeply rooted. (625)

Deep transformations have also affected the other class of socialist 211 society, the *peasantry*. Under capitalism, this was a class of small producers, very little in contact with each other, who lead a miserable life on their tiny plots. Life in the village resulted in cultural backwardness which often approximated savagery. Collectivization of agriculture and the cultural revolution have essentially changed the perspectives of the peasantry. . . . The socialist peasantry is a class free from exploitation by landowners and kulaks, and which works collectively with extensive use of machinery. Thanks to the kolhoz system, there is a rapid increase of cultural awareness of the peasantry. (625–626)

The *intelligentsia* is an important group in socialist society. . . . They 212 belong neither to the working class nor to the peasantry. And it is not a distinct class since it has no independent place in social production, although it plays a great role in the life of socialist society. . . . The intelligentsia is the fastest growing level of socialist society.[1] The specific importance of the intelligentsia will continue to grow, as demanded by the development of technology and culture. The socialist intelligentsia is not a separate social level, but a real intelligentsia of the people, brothers of the workers and peasants. It sees its highest goal in service to the people. (626)

By fully and finally ending the exploitation of man by man, socialism has 213 forever eliminated the century-old class-hierarchy, i.e. the system of the

[1] There were in the Soviet Union 190000 in 1913; 521000 in 1928 and 7500000 in 1958.

69

subordination of one class to another. All classes and levels are equal in their relations to means of production, to the state and political power, and in their rights and duties. No one can ever again seize the means of production and use them to exploit other men. This does not affect in the least the leadership role of the working class under socialism; for that role is based not on exclusive rights..., but on the high moral and political authority of the working class. (627)

214   From what has been said, it follows that under socialism the social distinctions do not disappear but change basic character. They are no longer bound up with relations of domination and subordination, but consist in differences between the separate, equal groups of workers, due to different forms of one and the same socialist property (property of the people and property of the cooperatives).... Therefore, under socialism the existing differences between the classes are basically different from those obtaining under capitalism, viz. they are non-antagonistic and decrease in the course of the development of the socialist society with the aid of the policies of the Party and state. (627–628)

215   Finally, the class differences under socialism also do not have as great an effect on the personal destiny of man as under capitalism.... In the socialist system the differences in the situations of men are due to personal qualities, abilities, knowledge and joy in work, not to their social origins and position.... Prestige and honor in socialist society are also no longer the monopoly of single classes and levels; they become the inalienable attributes of honorable service to society and of honorable work in every domain of activity. The mobility, the relativity of the limits between the classes of socialist society, and the ease of transition from one class or level to another lead to the elimination of class differences. (628)

216   As long as all classes and levels are made up of workers, and as long as all are related to a single – socialist – form of ownership, the relationships between them will be fully free from antagonism. Their interests coincide on everything basic and important.... Thus, socialism replaces the age-old fight of classes with solidarity and unity, resulting from common goals, ideology and morality. With the elimination of the exploiting classes and the socialist reformation of all petty bourgeois classes, the foundations are layed for the *moral-political unity* of society. (629)

SOCIALIST DEMOCRACY

With the disappearance of anti-worker classes, the state loses – as concerns 217
its internal functioning – the character of an instrument of class-oppression. (629) The disappearance of the class-oppression function does
not mean that the state must fade away under socialism. The socialist
society cannot get along without it.... First, because for a long time after
the victory of socialism the state remains the best and most rational form
of directing the economy, social relations and cultural construction....
Second, because under socialism there is still a certain inequality in the
satisfaction of man's needs, manifestations of private-ownership mentality,
and other remnants of capitalism in the consciousness of a section of the
members of society. Under such circumstances, one cannot do without a
special apparatus for the control of the accounting of work and consumption, for guarding personal and social property, and for restraining
anti-social acts.... Third, the state will be retained for external reasons.
As long as socialism has not reached world-wide proportions, there is
always the danger of attack by the imperialist states; whence the necessity
of armed forces and other governmental agencies to guarantee defence
and to fight against spies and other dangerous elements sent out by the
imperialists. (630)

Under socialism, therefore, the workers still need the state. Even the need 218
for a certain use of force by the state remains. But the primary functions
of the state lie elsewhere. In the first place, the *economic* role of the state
grows significantly.... The organization of social production and
direction of the economy become its most important functions. Also
greatly expanded is the cultural and educational role of the state, viz. its
activity in the development of socialist culture (science, art and literature),
and in the elevation of the cultural level of the people and its Communist
education. The state plays a large role in the *protecting of socialist
property*, ... of the rights and interests of the citizens, of their personal
property and of public order.... As long as the capitalist system exists
and the danger of a military attack is not eliminated, there remains the
job of *national defence* against external attack. (630–631)

Socialism creates for the first time the economic, social and political pre- 219
requisites for the realization of a democracy which really includes the

whole people. Only socialism creates a unity of interest of all levels of society such that all questions of public life can be democratically solved without class-determined force. Only under socialism is there a real political equality of all citizens. It is guaranteed by the fact that men are factually equal in reference to the means of production and have the right to collaborate in the elaboration of decisions which affect the whole society. (632)

220   Under socialism the members of society have not only formal rights and freedoms but also the practical possibility of using them. It is not by accident that the socialist constitutions, in speaking of the basic freedoms – freedom of speech, of the press, of meeting, of street demonstrations, etc. – put special emphasis on the guarantees which provide the practical possibility for use of these freedoms, i.e. they speak of providing paper, publishing facilities, meeting rooms, etc. for the workers. (632)

221   Of course, there is no question of unlimited personal freedom under socialism. . . . While the socialist state guarantees man the widest of freedoms, it at the same time forbids any activity aimed at hurting other men. It punishes, for example, the propagation of racist, fascist and militarist views. In distinction to the bourgeois state, the socialist state does not permit the distribution of valueless books, newspapers and films which harm youth and honor immorality, brutality and force. . . . Socialist democracy is not a democracy without direction, but a directed democracy – directed by the Party and state in the interests of the further development of socialism and the construction of Communism. (632–633)

222   An important characteristic of socialist democracy is the increasing importance of social organizations: the Party, the unions, the youth groups, etc. . . . The Marxist view of democracy gives great importance to political rights and freedoms but does not reduce democracy to this. For Marxists, a very important component of democracy is the social and social-economic rights of the workers: the right to work, to medical attention, to education, to material care in old-age and in illness, etc. These rights are the foundation of man's real freedom and happiness. (635)

223   One must not forget that socialism is only the first and lower phase of the new social formation. It is naturally not possible at this stage to completely

solve all the many difficult and complicated problems which the century-long reign of the exploiters has left to socialism. But it is already evident that socialism – as no other social order – guarantees to the worker real democratic rights and expands democracy to an unheard of extent. (637)

The elimination of national oppression and the successes in economic and cultural development have facilitated the transition of many peoples to nationhood, where this had earlier been denied them on the basis of their economic backwardness, administrative splintering, etc. (640) 224

THE CULTURE OF SOCIALIST SOCIETY

The socialist reorganization of society is inconceivable without profound changes in culture, which are rightly called the cultural revolution. The cultural revolution is not, however, to be understood in a vulgar sense as the negation of the whole preceding culture. Socialist culture ... is the rightful heir of the best of that which was created in the era of exploiter-society.... Another central task of the cultural revolution is the conversion of culture from a possession of the few to the property of the many. (641–642) 225

An absolutely necessary component of the cultural revolution in all countries is the transformation of the school from an instrument of class-domination by the bourgeoisie – which it was under capitalism – to an instrument of socialist re-education. The school will be separated from the church and freed from the influence of bourgeois ideology. Teaching will be gradually reformed on the basis of scientific knowledge proved by experience. A new system of popular education will be fashioned. It forms educated men who are armed with basic scientific and technological knowledge and who are able to collaborate in socialist construction. (643) 226

In order to ensure such a growth and to assure a rise in forces of production and culture in society, the cultural revolution must without fail accomplish another important task, i.e. the creation of a new and truly popular intelligentsia which is closely bound up with the working class and the peasantry. The task ... is accomplished in two ways: by the attraction and re-education of the bourgeois intelligentsia and by the accelerated 227 formation of professionals from the ranks of the workers and peasants. (643)

228   Writers, artists and actors do not have to worry under socialism about lack of public attention. . . . Rapid social progress, constant rise in the cultural level of the masses and in the well-being of the people, and scientifically founded confidence in the future – all of this constitutes an extraordinarily favorable climate for creative work. This places, of course, great responsibility on the artist. Literature and art do not only reflect the life of the people, they also help to form the human soul. . . . Artistic creation cannot remain outside the class-war and outside of politics because every writer and artist, whether he likes it or not, expresses in his work the interests of some class. (645–646) The main requirement of socialist realism is that reality be truly presented in its progressive development. The important Party document "For a close binding of literature and art with the life of the people" says: "Under the conditions of socialist society, where the people really is free, is the real lord of its fate and the creator of a new life, there is for the artist who truly serves his people no question as to whether he is free or not free in his work. For such an artist, it is evident how he is to approach reality – he does not have to conform or to force himself. The true representation of life from the standpoint of Communist partymindedness is close to his heart: he stands firm on this position, represents it and defends it in his work." This is exactly how the socialist intellectuals conceive their profession. (647)

SOCIALISM AND THE INDIVIDUAL

229   The bourgeois critics of socialist society try to prove that it is irreconcilable with individual freedom. They claim that revolutionary Marxism recognizes no value in the human person. Hundreds of books and thousands of articles have been written about the "totalitarian" nature of socialist society, about the "absorption of the person by the collectivity" and about the "levelling" of man. Nothing could be more false. (647)

230   Man cannot have freedom from society: freedom is possible only in society. In order to free the person, one must free all men by changing

the social relations by which they were enslaved. . . . Socialism is the first to recognize the simple workers' right to development and to independent creativity – the simple workers who had always been considered condescendingly by bourgeois ideologists as the "dismal mass". At the same time, it guarantees this right by putting in the hands of society all the material means for developing the talents and capabilities of man. (648–649)

Socialist society is, above all, occupied by general interests. But, it is **231** responsible not only for the well-being of the whole society but also for that of each member. Therefore, socialist morality condemns all manifestations of individualism and small-owner egoism, judging them rightly to be remnants of the capitalist past in man's consciousness. On the other hand, F. Engels already pointed out that "society cannot free itself without freeing each individual". Care for man and a sensitive and attentive relationship to him is one of the most important demands of socialist morality. Under socialism, every member of society can improve his situation, through productive and qualified work. It is natural that man's efforts to increase his well-being in this way correspond to the interests of society and are supported by it. . . . As socialist consciousness grows in the popular masses, the moral drives begin to play an ever greater role in the conduct of men and solicitude for social affairs becomes the personal matter of every man. (649–650)

Of course, it is impossible in a few decades to uproot all ideas and habits **232** which have been implanted by centuries of domination by private property. There are still in the consciousness of many members of socialist society many character traits of the old morality and way of life: a less conscientious attitude toward work, greed, egoism, national prejudices, false attitudes toward women, alcoholism, and anti-social views which often lead to rowdyism and crime. . . . For this reason, there remains – even after the victory of socialism – the necessity for the consequent and daily work of education. Socialism is unthinkable without that social discipline which obliges the citizens to conform to society's requirements and to follow the rules of socialist life in common. . . . The self-developing unity of personal and social interests is the most important moral advantage of the socialist order, wherein the old tragedy of the "inner strife" of human consciousness is eliminated, thus shaping men who are whole, lively and hearty, and without fear of difficulties. The victory of socialism leads to the greatest revolution in morality. (650–651)

THE MOTIVE FORCES OF THE DEVELOPMENT OF SOCIALIST SOCIETY

233 With the victory of socialism, progressive development of society is not halted, but accelerated. In a quick tempo – unthinkable for previous formations – is completed the development of industry and agriculture, of social and political relations, of the whole social superstructure, and its perfection in the direction of Communism. . . . Society is forever freed from antagonisms. The contradictions of its development have become non-antagonistic. They are essentially contradictions and difficulties of growth, bound up with the tremendous ascent of socialist society and the even more quickly rising needs of men; contradictions which come to be with the shock of the new and the old, the progressive and the backward. (651)

234 Such contradictions are not solved in class-war – in socialist society there are no social levels or classes which would be interested in halting development and defending the old, backward orders – but in the collaboration of all classes and levels which are equally interested in the strengthening of socialism and the construction of Communism. Criticism and self-criticism forms the best means for laying bare and solving these contradictions. Where criticism is stifled, there is a standstill and the necessary resolution of contradictions is rendered difficult. (651)

235 Freedom from antagonistic contradictions is a tremendous advantage of socialist society. . . . In the development of society an ever greater role is played by those factors which do not divide men and bring them in conflict one with the other, but (which) bring them together and bind them in the achievement of common goals. . . . *Collective work* on the basis of socialist property becomes an extraordinary motive force of social development. . . . Collective work and comradely mutual help and collaboration produce *socialist competition* – which arouses and develops all of man's capabilities – as a new form of creative collaboration. . . . Thanks to the basic change which class-relations undergo with the victory of socialism, a firm foundation is provided for the *moral-political unity* of society. This unity of all classes and social levels – as to their main

interests – also becomes a powerful motive force of social development. . . . Another important motive force of socialist society is the friendship of socialist nations both within the country and in the socialist world-system. . . . The high ideational qualities of the socialist person are also expressed in the activating sentiment of socialist patriotism. (652–653)

A very important peculiarity of social development under socialism is the fact that it loses its elemental character and becomes a process in which the planned, conscious activity of man plays an ever greater role. This is why the Marxist-Leninist Party, . . . as the most perfect and all-round incorporation of the collective intellect and will of socialist society, is so important. The correct and clever leadership of the Party is the necessary condition for the use of all possibilities and advantages of the socialist system. Therefore, Marxist-Leninists attribute great importance, even after the victory of socialism, to strengthening the leadership role of the Party and to increasing its specific influence in all domains of social life. (654)   236

Chapter 25

THE SOCIALIST WORLD-SYSTEM

The conditions necessary for the formation of a world-system came to be only in the era of capitalism, when the development of the forces of production tied tightly together the economies of different countries. . . . The formation of a capitalist world-system was the result of uninterrupted fighting in all its forms: military, political, economic and ideological. . . . The capitalist world-system is a strict hierarchy. . . . It resembles a pyramid with a handful of developed powers on top and the vast majority of the backward and oppressed peoples on the bottom. (656–657)   237

The socialist world-system is completely different. It is not a hierarchy based on subordination and dependence, but a friendship group of free and equal states. . . . The historical mission of the working class fundamentally conditions other ways and means for the formation of the socialist world-system. The working class does not destroy exploitation and oppression in its own country just to preserve or re-establish it in the international field. The path to the formation of the socialist world-system is the way to a free association of equal peoples and not the subordination of the weak to the strong. (657)   238

239   The socialist world-system ... serves to foster the fastest development of all countries belonging to it and the elevation of the backward countries to the level of the developed. The existence of this system renders the construction of socialism in any country economically possible, irrespective of its degree of development at the moment of revolution. Earlier, this possibility existed only for countries which had attained at least a medium stage of economic development. This factor is important for insufficiently developed countries. The socialist world-system is a staunch guarantee of the security of each of its members in the face of the imperialist camp and, thereby, creates the political possibility for the construction of socialism in any country irrespective of its size, population or military potential. (657)

240   The economy of each socialist land develops as an independent national economy.... As characteristic and typical of socialism as the blossoming of nations is the association of nations and peoples, the collaboration of the national economic systems, and the ever further progressing association of socialist nations. (659) No one can better know the needs and possibilities of a socialist nation than it itself; no one can better view the particularities of its economic, political and cultural development than it itself. Therefore, every interference from outside – even when well intentioned – is not only out of place but can harm the socialist construction of a country. (661)

241   Although each socialist country is a sovereign state, it cannot retire within its national boundaries and ignore the methods which other lands use to solve the problems of socialism. (661) The national interests of the socialist states are in harmony with their common interests and goals. (662)

242   True internationalists must constantly have in mind that the distortion of the role of the Soviet Union in the socialist camp has a special place in the arsenal of contemporary reaction and nationalism. Capitalist propaganda and its revisionists seconds ... maintain, for example, that the Soviet Union "directs" the other socialist lands and that their Communist Parties are "dependent" on the CPSU.... In reality the role of the Soviet Union in the socialist world-system has nothing in common with that presented in inimical propaganda. In the Communist movement there are no "more highly placed" and "subordinate" Parties, just as there are

no "ruling states" and "satellites" in the socialist camp. All socialist lands are fully independent in the solution of their national problems and each of them has an equal voice in solution of common problems of the socialist camp. In the same way, the Communist and Workers' Parties are fully independent and equal; they are responsible to the workers of their own land and to the whole international workers' movement, but not to the Party of any one land. The Communist Party of the Soviet Union has no claim at all to the leadership role in the international Communist movement. Thus it is incorrect to speak of the leadership of the Soviet Union in the socialist camp.... Thanks to its rich experience, it simply gives an example of the fight for socialism and of the successful solution of the extremely complex tasks of socialist and Communist construction. (665)

When the Soviet Union was building socialism, it found itself in a capitalist 243 encirclement and had to create an all-round industrial system with only its internal resources and its own work-force. This determined the specific form of the Soviet socialist industrialization. The newly established socialist lands do not have to achieve such an autarchy. They are able to use the formidable advantages of the international socialist division of labor. (668) It is completely understandable that the socialist lands are interested in a long-range planning of their foreign trade relations.... The socialist world-market, where trade is planned for some years ahead, is subject to no depressions. It has no marketing difficulties, trade barriers and limits, no regional groups and preferential tariffs. The volume of this market constantly grows under the influence of planned specialization and cooperation in production in the context of the socialist world-system. (672)

Chapter 26

THE PERIOD OF TRANSITION FROM SOCIALISM
TO COMMUNISM

Despite all of its enormous accomplishments, the socialist social order is 244 only the first stage of that new, just society, the establishment of which is the final goal of the working class. Therefore, the workers – once having established socialism – forge, under the leadership of the Marxist-

Leninist Party, ahead to the construction of Communism.... There is no wall between socialism and Communism. They are not two different types of society, but two phases of one and the same social formation, which differ as to their degree of maturity. (677)

THE GENERAL LINE OF THE PARTY

245 The policy developed by the Party sees the solution of the main tasks of this period as follows:

All-round development of the forces of production, which assures the creation of the material-technical base of Communism; the greatest possible acceleration of technological progress; uninterrupted increase in work-productivity and, on this basis, the constant elevation of the living standard of the people; achievement of the superiority of the U.S.S.R. in peaceful, economic competition with the most highly developed capitalist lands; strengthening of socialist state-property; higher development of cooperative-collective property in agriculture to the level of general state-property; gradual overcoming of the distinction between city and country, between spiritual and manual labor and, on this basis, the gradual elimination of the class-differences and other social distinctions in Soviet society; intensification of ideational-educational work; overcoming the remnants of capitalism in the consciousness of man; increase of the Communist consciousness of the workers; further perfecting of the socialist, Soviet order; development of socialist democracy; expansion of the field of activity of social organizations; development of the activity and initiative of the broad popular masses; consequent accomplishment of a foreign policy of establishing world-peace on the basis of the Leninist principle of peaceful coexistence of lands with different social systems; strengthening of the socialist world-system. (680)

THE CREATION OF THE MATERIAL-TECHNICAL BASE OF COMMUNISM

246 The transition to Communism is unthinkable without a surplus of material and spiritual goods: industrial products, food, living quarters, cultural goods and rest-homes for the workers. This presumes a gigantic growth of production in all branches of industry, agriculture, transport and construction.... The main direction in the fight for a rapid growth of

production is the completion of the automation of all labor processes and the elimination of all manual labor from all branches of the national economy.... While mechanization frees man from the burden of heavy physical work, automation frees him from unnecessary nervous tension. (683) Only in this way can the production-technology of Communism be created, the goal of which is to complete the liberation of man from heavy, monotonous work and conserve his spiritual energy for creative ends. (684–685)

The newest technology and scientific discoveries, no matter how 247 astounding they are, cannot by themselves lead to basic transformations in industry and agriculture. In order to gain full advantage for the national economy ... a good organization of work is necessary. (691) An important factor in the organization of work is the structure of the administration of the economy.... One side of the problem is the decentralization of the direction of the economy; the other, is amelioration of the methods of centralized planning and coordination of all branches and domains of the economy. The central planning institutions (the importance of which incessantly increases, when the increased complexity of the economy demands a more exact coordination of the specialized areas of the economy) will gradually change from administrative institutions to scientific-technical councils. (693)

The transition to the technology of Communism also changes the character 248 of work, the production-readiness of man, and his spiritual world. Full mechanization and automation already lead to the repression of less qualified work.... Work on automated lines is like that of engineers.... The general educational and cultural level of the workers grows apace. (693)

Thus, in the process of socialist production the new physiognomy of the 249 worker – typical for the future Communist society – is created. He is a conscious and educated, highly qualified specialist in his domain with a wide technical view (of other domains). Gradually, too, becomes evident the path along which will be found the solution to that great problem of mankind, viz. the liberation of man from the old enslaving division of work.... Then appear the prerequisites for the ever easier transition of the worker from one sphere of production to another. And this means that life-long attachment to one single profession will be eliminated; a situation which – as Marx said – has lead to the oppression of the whole world of spiritual capacities of man. (694)

THE OVERCOMING OF CLASS-DIFFERENCES

250 Under socialism, as said, there are still classes, the working class and the peasantry. This is due to the simultaneous presence of two forms of social property, to the further existence of differences between city and country, and to the persistence of different forms of the division of material goods. Under socialism there also remains the division of society into men who do spiritual work and those who do manual labor. (695) The whole development of collective property leads to an ever higher level of its socialization. In character it approximates the level of general state property. In the future, the coalescence of these two forms of ownership to a single Communist form is historically unavoidable. (689)

251 The differences between workers and peasants are not bound up only with the existence of the two forms of social property. Some little importance is to be attributed to the differences in character of industrial and agricultural production and the differences in living conditions and cultural level.... The main task is to overcome the backwardness of the village in comparison to the town. The technological revolution in agriculture ... basically changes the character of farm work, changing it always more into a type of industrial work. (699)

252 On the road to Communism, the division of society into manual and spiritual laborers is also to be overcome.... The main role in this is played by the changes in the character of work itself, which ... demands from men an ever more constant intellectual growth, a wide-ranging view, extensive knowledge and a creative approach.... Technological progress is the most important motive force in the process of bringing together manual and spiritual work. But it would be incorrect to believe that this progress could by itself lead to overcoming the differences between them. In capitalist countries mechanization and automation lead very often to a decrease in the importance of the worker in the process and to his conversion to an appendage of the "clever" machine. This is excluded in socialist countries where technological progress

82

unfolds under other social conditions and where the worker actively takes part in the direction of production. Here, society is constantly solicitous that the worker does not become a robot, but an all-round developed and cultivated man, creator and master of technology. Under socialism, the whole system of general and professional education serves this end. (702)

An important part of the overcoming of the differences between spiritual and manual labor falls to socialism's system of popular education.... Naturally, the elimination of the dividing line between the intelligentsia, on the one hand, and the worker and peasant, on the other, is a lengthy process, much longer than the overcoming of the differences between the workers and peasants. (703)   253

As long as the differences between spiritual and manual laborers exist the highly qualified portion of the intelligentsia receives salaries higher than those of the simple workers and peasants. With the approach to Communism, the differences in salary . . . gradually disappear. There is, of course, no question of egalitarianism in salaries: this is an objective process. In the course of the mechanization of the various branches of the national economy, work becomes ever more homogeneous, viz. qualified work in controlling machines, and this naturally leads to the equalization of salaries. (705) Further, with the general rise of wages, the remuneration of the lower and middle workers and clerks will be significantly increased. (706)   254

Particularly favorable perspectives are opened up by the increase of those material goods which society will distribute not according to work done but gratuitously or as bonuses, and which form the fund of social consumption. With this fund, society meets the expenses for social and cultural needs: construction, health care, education, child care, sport. From this fund, will be financed social security, scholarships, help for large families, etc. (706)   255

The ideal of many men in capitalist society is to have as many goods as possible in their private possession: their own house, their own car, etc. Naturally, such goods are not available for all and they tend to be concentrated at the higher levels of society. It would be a vulgar conception of socialism to say that it simply intends that each citizen should have his own house and car. Socialism knows the faster and more reasonable way   256 to achievement of general well-being. This is the concentration of ever more goods and services in the hands of society which gradually assumes responsibility for the satisfaction of the needs of the citizens for these goods and services.[1] (707)

COMMUNIST EDUCATION OF THE WORKER

257 The complex process of the gradual transition from socialism to Communism also includes profound changes in the mode of life, in the spiritual superstructure of society, and in the consciousness and mores of men. The Communist Party takes this into account in its efforts for the Communist education of workers and tries to accelerate this law-bound process as much as possible. Communist education includes such important elements as: elevation of the education level and professional knowledge of the members of society; elevation of general culture; growth of the Communist consciousness of the workers; transformation of work to the common weal of society, and of conformation to the norms and rules of Communist morality, and of virtue to a habit. (708) This will provide a new *cultural revolution* rendering man more educated and cultivated. (709)

258 The Communist Party is conscious that its world-view is the possession not only of the vanguard, the progressive portion, of the workers, peasants and intelligentsia, but also will be that of all members of society. (711) Important for ideological training are fine literature, radio, television, theater, films and the plastic arts. These carry the high ideals of Communism to the broadest popular masses and in a form which affects not only the reason but also the sentiments of man and, therefore, is particularly impressive. (712)

259 In ideological training one meets difficulties and obstacles with which one must unrelentingly fight. These are the remnants of capitalism in the consciousness of a portion of mankind and the nefarious influence of bourgeois ideology which is harmful to Communist construction. The final overcoming of these remnants is an important task of the transitional period to Communism. It is above all necessary to completely erase such remains of the past as the false attitude toward social property and work,

---

[1] For economic reasons it is better, e.g., to keep cars in social garages.

nationalism, and religious prejudices, alcoholism, denigration of women and uncontrolled conduct. (712)

In the course of the development toward Communism there will be an increase not only in the demands of the members of society but also in the demands of society on its citizens, regarding their conduct in production, in public, in the family and in home life. These demands, however, will depend more and more on moral persuasion and conviction. At the same time, main responsibility for the education of the new man will fall to the collectivity. . . . There can be no doubt that it is precisely in the collectivity that the man of the future – the man for whom the principles of Communism form the foundation of consciousness and the voice of conscience – is formed. (715)   260

THE DEVELOPMENT OF SOCIALIST DEMOCRACY

The development and perfecting of socialist democracy is a particularly important task of the transitional period to Communism. (715) The further development of democracy means, above all, constant perfecting of the structure and work methods of the state institutions, and strengthening of their bond with the broad masses. The political system will be formed so that workers will have an ever greater possibility of directly participating in state matters. . . . Especially important for the development of socialist democracy is the practice of general popular discussion of law projects and decrees of the state, and of the most important questions of economic and cultural construction. . . . Characteristic of the transitional period to Communism will be the gradual extension of the rights of local organs. (716–717) A fundamentally new direction in the development of democracy, appearing in the transitional period to Communism, is the step by step passage of governmental powers to social organizations. (718)   261

The development of socialist democracy is simultaneously the process of laying the foundations for the withering away of the state. . . . Concretely, the withering away of the state means first of all, the gradual disappearance of a special group of men, constantly occupied with the state and really forming the state, and their reabsorption into society. In other words, the withering away of the state presupposes the constant decrease and final   262 elimination of the state apparatus and the transferal of its functions to society itself, i.e. to the social organizations and to the whole people. Second, the withering away of the state means the gradual disappearance of the necessity of the use of force against the members of society.... But it does not mean that in the future there will be no administrative apparatus. The necessity of administering social production will always exist, but this will be done not by a state but by *social self-administration.* ... Social self-administration is the result of the development and perfecting of socialist democracy. One can, therefore, say that the process of the withering away of the state is already under way. (720–721) The question on the withering away of the state must not be seen in isolation from the international situation.... As long as there is the danger of imperialist aggression, those organs of the state which serve for protection from external enemies should not be weakened. (722)

263 A characteristic trait of the development of socialist democracy during the transitional period to Communism is the increasing importance of the Communist Party as the orienting and directing force.... As already said, the construction of Communist society follows objective laws but is not, for all this, automatic. (723) As the state gradually transfers many of its functions to social organizations, the Party comes more and more into the spotlight as the directive force of the whole society and as the directive force of all social organizations. The Party directs the process of the withering away of the state as well as the activity of the unions and other social organizations, and helps them take the new places which are theirs on the road to Communism. (724)

264 It is presumed that the increased importance of the Party brings with it higher demands.... In the period of the all-around construction of Communism, many of the measures of yesterday have lost their validity. Today, the higher demands require successes which are faster, easier and less strenuous. (724)

THE INTERNATIONAL SIGNIFICANCE OF COMMUNIST
CONSTRUCTION IN THE U.S.S.R.

265 On the way toward Communism the Soviet Union faces the great eco-

nomic victory over capitalism. This is the accomplishment of the main economic task of the U.S.S.R. It means the overtaking in an historically short time, of the pro capita production of the most highly developed capitalist lands. (727)

Life has now posed a new question of basic theoretical and practical importance, which concerns the development of socialist countries toward Communism. The 21st Congress of the CPSU answered this question. In N. S. Khrushchov's speech we find: "It is theoretically more correct to assume that the socialist lands – with successful use of the inner capacities of the socialist order – will enter the higher phase of Communist society more or less simultaneously." (730)   266

The successes of the economic and political development of the socialist camp make possible a new approach to the question on the perspectives for the progress of mankind toward Communism.... Up to now, the bourgeoisie was able to speculate on the deficiencies and difficulties in the construction of the new society. Such speculations are done. The day is near when the workers of the Soviet Union will have the shortest working day, the shortest working week and the highest living standard in the world. Together with the successes in the development of socialist democracy and culture, this shows the broad working masses of the capitalist lands, in the most clear and convincing form, the advantages of the socialist system. The power of attraction of Marxism-Leninism increases.... All of this widens and strengthens the front of forces which come out for the transition to a new social order. The process of the social liberation of the workers speeds up. In particular, the prospects of a peaceful transition to socialism become ever more real. (732–733)   267

When the Soviet Union, through its successes in Communist construction, has become the strongest economic power and the camp of socialism has surpassed the capitalist world in volume of industrial production, the effect on the underdeveloped lands of Asia, Africa and Latin America will be profound. And the help which the socialist camp can give them in overcoming economic and cultural backwardness will be even more effective.   268

Chapter 27

ON COMMUNIST SOCIETY

269 Communism is that society which once and for all puts an end to need and poverty and guarantees well-being for all its citizens. The working man's age-old dream of plenty becomes reality. . . . Man's first care was always his care for daily bread. Communism finally and forever solves this problem. (735) The higher the level of civilization, the more numerous and diverse are the things and services which men want. Already today well-being includes not only good food but also comfortable and spacious dwellings, well-made and attractive clothes and various consumer goods which facilitate and beautify existence. Included are comfortable means of transport, objects for cultivated leisure (books, radio, television sets, musical instruments, sporting goods) and a series of other things. Communism takes as its goal the full satisfaction of men in respect to all these goods and services. (736)

FROM EACH ACCORDING TO HIS CAPABILITIES

270 Under Communism as in any other social order, the sole source of all values remains human work. . . . No matter how developed technology becomes and how many victories science achieves, the unshakeable principle of Communist society remains: from each according to his capabilities. (738)

271 The material drives (salary for work) have a decisive importance in socialist society, where they work together with the moral drives. Under Communism, all members of society will do their work strictly for moral motives, thanks to their advanced consciousness. In other words, there will be gratis work with gratis satisfaction of all of the workers' needs. (738) Of course, work becomes a habit and a vital need of each man not just because men have achieved a higher consciousness, but also because the character of work itself has changed. . . . Under Communism human work will be definitively freed from all that has made it a burden for centuries. It becomes not only free but also really creative. (739)

272 Every worker performs . . . functions which are now done by engineers; men devote twenty to twenty-five hours a week to production . . . and,

in time, even less; every man can choose his occupation according to his tendencies and capabilities; all talents and capabilities hidden in man are fully developed and applied either in the process of production or during leisure time; during his work, he does not have to think about his wages – about how much he will be payed – because society takes full care of the satisfaction of his needs; work enjoys the highest respect of society and is the ultimate measure of a man's worth. (739–740)

TO EACH ACCORDING TO HIS NEEDS

Communism introduces a form of the division of material and spiritual 273
goods based on the principle, to each according to his needs. In other words, irrespective of his position and the quantity or quality of the work he gives to society, a man receives all he needs without counterpart. . . . The possibility of always receiving gratis from the stocks of society whatever is necessary for a cultivated and comfortable life leads to a healing of the whole human psyche which no longer suffers under cares about tomorrow. In the new psyche and new morality there will be no place for worries about income and private property, the chase after which was the whole sense of many men's lives under capitalism. Man finally has the possibility of devoting himself to higher interests, the first of which are those of society. (741)

Of course, Communist society cannot take upon itself the satisfaction of 274
extravagant wishes and whims. Its goal, as Engels stressed, is the satisfaction of the reasonable needs of man, in an ever increasing measure. . . . Men will of themselves be sufficiently cultivated and conscious as not to make unreasonable demands on society. . . . It takes some time, of course, to educate all men to a reasonable attitude toward consumption, but it is not to be doubted that the society of the future, with its surplus of material and spiritual goods and with the high degree of consciousness of its citizens, will be fully up to this task. (742)

THE FREE MAN IN A FREE SOCIETY

Communism is the most just of social orders, for in it the principles of 275
equality and freedom are fully realized, the blossoming of human personality is guaranteed, and society is changed into a well-ordered

union and a community of creative men.... Equality is achieved above all, because Communism is a classless society in which the last remains of social distinction and the inequality accompanying it – which still remained under socialism, like the differences between city and country, between manual and spiritual workers – are eliminated. The disappearance of these differences by no means implies a levelling of individuals or an equalization of human capacities and character. Communism is not a military camp peopled with characterless figures.... In reality, this society includes unheard of room for the unlimited blossoming of human individuality in all of its endless diversity. (744)

276   Communist equality does not presuppose the elimination of all differences between men but only those differences and conditions which can cause a difference in the social situation and position of men. Irrespective of the origins and positions of a man and of his contribution to social production, he receives under Communism the same possibility as all others for participation in the deciding of common affairs, for self-development and for use of all goods. (744)

At the same time, Communism brings the full triumph of human freedom.... By transforming production, distribution and work, Communism guarantees full fusion of the social-economic interests of all members of society. Consequently, all grounds for the use of force disappear. The relations of domination and subordination are finally dissolved by free work in common. The necessity for a state disappears. The need for jurisprudential regulation vanishes. For the cultivated, spiritual and morally developed man – to which level men have developed under Communism – following the rules of human community life has become a habit, second nature. (745)

PEACE BETWEEN PEOPLES

277   Communism leads to new relationships between peoples. (748) Of course, nations and, consequently, national cultures and languages will remain in existence long after the victory of Communism. But the life and contact between different peoples will be freed from everything which might give the least occasion for enmity and discord, for separation and conflict, for national egoism and national limitations. (749)

VIEW INTO THE DISTANT FUTURE OF COMMUNISM

But when men have reached this peak, they will not remain there, contented and in contemplation. On the contrary, their energy will be multiplied. In place of the solved tasks, new ones appear and, when one goal is reached, new and more enticing ones are set. The wheel of history will continue to turn. (751–752) Above all, it is certain that the development of social production will never come to a halt. What are the factors which will foster uninterrupted progress? First, the constant and very rapid growth of human needs in Communist society; further, the growth of the population; ... and the social need of further shortening of the work-time of the workers and increase of their leisure time will work in the same direction. (752) 278

Science, which has an important place in Communist society, will be presented with ever new problems.[1] 279

There are no limits to man's inquisitive spirit, for his efforts to put the forces of nature to work for him and to uncover all of its secrets. In addition, there is no respite for human activity which is directed toward the perfecting of the structure of the society in which they live – the forms of social self-rule and the norms of human life in common and of human intercourse. And what an inexhaustible field of activity opens up before Communist society, when it is a question of the development of the capacities and blossoming of the personality of all of its members, and of the physical and spiritual perfecting of man himself! (753) 280

---

[1] The well-known Soviet scholar and member of the Academy, V. A. Obručev, ... writes: "It is imperative: to extend man's average lifespan to 150 or 200 years; to eliminate infectious diseases and reduce the non-infectious to a minimum; to overcome old-age and fatigue; to bring back life in cases of early, unnatural death; to put into the service of man all the forces of nature – the sun, winds, underground heat, etc. – and to use atomic energy in industry, transport and building; to predict and render henceforward innocuous natural catastrophes such as tidal waves, hurricanes, volcanic eruptions and earthquakes; ..." (752)

SUBJECT-INDEX

The numbers refer to the serially numerated paragraphs.

FREEDOM, and the dictatorship of the proletariat 171; bourgeois 32, 134, 135; in art 228; limits of 221; under Communism 276; under socialism 220, 229–232

HIERARCHY, under capitalism 237; under socialism 213–216, 238
HISTORY, content of 26
HUMANISM, and dictatorship of the proletariat 167; of the intelligentsia 145; of the working class 157, 166

IDEAS, as element of superstructure 25; meaning of – in history 37
IDEOLOGY, and the Marxist-Leninist Party 122; and the people 258–260; as internationalism of working class 104
IMPERIALISM (df.) 65, 66; 95; American 78, 130, 131, 137; as political reaction 72; division of the world under 69, 70; parasitic nature of 71; state system of 237; war, danger of 79, 84, 137–140, 142
IMPOVERISHMENT, s. wages
INDIVIDUALISM, of the socialist intelligentsia 210; rejection of 231
INTELLIGENTSIA, as allies of the worker 100, 102, 106, 145; the new 227; place of – under socialism 212; under capitalism 90, 91, 102; under Communism 252, 254, 272
INTERNATIONALISM 104

KNOWLEDGE, as reflection 19

LAW (df.) 9; of social development 35–39
LEADERSHIP, in history 47; of the Party, s. party
LEAP, in dialectical development 12
LIFE 5

MARKET, and anarchy 194; and crises 58–60; fight for 69, 70, 77
MASS-ORGANIZATIONS, lead by the Party 175; under socialist democracy 222; under Communism 262, 263
MATERIALISM 3; function of 7; historical 22
MATTER (df.) 4; forms of 5; in the life of society 23
MEANS OF PRODUCTION, capitalist 32, 33, 53–64; historical forms of 26–34; in transition to Communism 246–249; socialist 194–208
MIDDLE CLASSES, s. petty bourgeoisie
MILITARIZATION, of the economy 84
MONOPOLY 67; as anti-democratic 145; of the state 81–85
MORALITY, during the transition to Communism 260; socialist 231, 232; under Communism 273, 274, 276
MOTION, as attribute of matter 5

NATION 40 (note); in transition to Communism 266; sovereignty of 132, 133; under capitalism 237; under Communism 277; under socialism 224, 240, 241
NATIONALIZATION, capitalist 83; of monopolies 145; socialist 185

NATURE, laws of 39; man's control over 49, 280; objective existence of 2; priority of 3

NECESSITY, and chance 9; blind and guided 38; historical 35; of the disappearance of capitalism 93–95

NEEDS, as basis of production 23; equality of 264; in primitive society 27; under capitalism 57, 60; under Communism 246, 255, 256, 272–274; under socialism 201, 208, 218

NEGATION, dialectical 16

OPPORTUNISM 108, 122, 123, 169

OPPOSITIONS, fight of 14; s. contradiction, class-differences

OPTIMISM 18

OVER-PRODUCTION 58–60

PACIFISM 138

PARTY, and democratic centralism 111–116; and the masses (leadership) 117, 119, 126, 175; and ideological purity 122–124; and unity of purpose 114–116, 176; as part of superstructure 25; as revolutionary 108, 109; in anti-capitalist class-war 107, 109, 125, 126, 136, 138; in the dicatatorship of the proletariat 173–176, 179, 180; in the socialist revolution 147, 153, 155; in the transition to Communism 263, 264; Marxist-Leninist 107–124; meaning of theory and politics as science and art for 110, 120, 121; needs leaders 47; relations with other parties 242; under socialism 221, 236

PARTYMINDEDNESS of art 228, 258

PATRIOTISM, socialist 235

PEACE, as socialist policy 138, 140; fight for 137–141, 145; revolution in 158; under Communism 277

PEASANT, and cooperatives 187, 188; as ally of the worker 128; in the transition to Communism 250, 251; under feudalism 30; under capitalism 88, 89, 101, 127; under socialism 211

PERSON, under Communism 275, 276, 280; under socialism 229–232

PERSONALITY-CULT 47

PETTY BOURGEOISIE 88, 89; as ally of the working class 100, 101

PHILOSOPHY, basic question of 3; character of Marxist-Leninist 1

PLANNED ECONOMY, under capitalism 194; under Communism 247; under socialism 194, 195, 203, 204

POPULAR DEMOCRACY 180, 181

POPULAR MASSES, in the socialist revolution 151; in power 170, 172; role in history 46, 47

POWER 154

PRIMITIVE SOCIETY 27

PRODUCTION, elements of 23; development of 24, 45

PROFIT, as motive force of capitalist production 54, 55, 57

PROGRESS 17; in exploiter society 50, 51; social 48–52; under Communism 278–280; under socialism 52

PROLETARIAT, s. working class, dictatorship of the proletariat

PROPERTY RELATIONS 24; and social equality 213, 216; as basis of the social structure 25, 41; in transition to Communism 250; in transition to socialism 184–189, 193; under capitalism 53, 92; under socialism 196–199

QUALITY, and quantity 10, 11

RACE 40 (note)
REALISM, socialist 228
REFLECTION (cognitive) 19
REFORMISM 45, 169
REGRESSION 18, 50
RELIGION, as element of superstructure 25; in fight for peace 138; overcoming of 259
REVISIONISM 123, 161, 242
REVOLUTION, and power 45, 154; as basic form of social transition 45; democratic 146–148; laws of socialist 161; material prerequisites of 191; peaceful and violent 155–160; socialist 142–161

SECTARIANISM 124
SLAVE-HOLDING SOCIETY 28, 29
SOCIAL FORMATIONS 27–34; history as series of 26; inner structure of 25
SOCIALIZATION of means of the production, s. nationalization
SOCIALISM 34, 194–243; culture under 225–228; freedom and person under 229–232; means of production in 194–208; non-antagonistic 214, 216, 233–235; social progress under 52, 233, 236; social structure of 209–216; state and political life under 217–224; world-system of 227–234
SOVEREIGNTY, defense of 145; of socialist states 240–242
STATE, capitalist 177; — capitalism in transition to socialism 189; functions of 42; –monopoly capitalism 81–83; origins of 28; –property under capitalism 83; –property under socialism 197; the socialist 217–219; types of 43; under dictatorship of the proletariat 162–183; withering away of the 262
STRATEGY, and tactics 120
SUPERSTRUCTURE 25

THEORY, importance of – for the Marxist-Leninist Party 120–124
TRANSITIONAL PERIOD, and the withering away of the state 261–264; creation of the material base of 246–249; economic measures in 184–193; education of workers in 257–260; from capitalism to socialism 162–194; from socialism to Communism 244–269; international implications of 265–269; main tasks of 245; overcoming of class-differences during 250–256; results of 193; the state in 172–183
TRUTH, absolute and relative 19

USA 78, 137
UNEMPLOYMENT 59, 87
UPRISING, armed 156, 157, 159

SOVIETICA

Publications and Monographs of the Institute of East-European Studies,
University of Fribourg, Switzerland; edited by J. M. Bocheński
and published by D. Reidel Publishing Company, Dordrecht-Holland.

PUBLICATIONS

Bibliographie der sowjetischen Philosophie. Heft I, 1959, VIII + 72 S., ƒ 12.25. Heft II, 1959, IV + 109 S., ƒ 15.75. Heft III, 1962, X + 73 S., ƒ 18.50. Heft IV, 1963, XII + 161 S., ƒ 28.75. Heft V, 1964, VI + 143 S., ƒ 26.50.

BALLESTREM, KARL G.: *Russian Philosophical Terminology* (Russian – English – German – French). 1964, VIII + 116 pp., ƒ 20.00.

BIRJUKOV, B. V.: *Two Soviet Studies on Frege.* Translated and edited by I. Angelelli. 1964, XXII + 101 pp., ƒ 18.00.

BLAKELEY, T. J.: *Soviet Philosophy.* A General Introduction to Contemporary Soviet Thought. 1964, VI + 82 pp., ƒ 16.00.

BOCHEŃSKI, J. M.: *Die dogmatischen Grundlagen der sowjetischen Philosophie, Stand 1958.* Zusammenfassung der *Osnovy marksistskoj filosofii* mit Register. 1959, XII + 84 S., ƒ 12.50.
The Dogmatic Principles of Soviet Philosophy (as of 1958). Synopsis of the *Osnovy marksistskoj filosofii* with complete index. 1963, XII + 78 pp., ƒ 15.00.

FLEISCHER, HELMUT: *Kleines Textbuch der kommunistischen Ideologie.* Auszüge aus dem Lehrbuch *Osnovy marksizma-leninizma* mit Register. 1963, XIV + 116 S., ƒ 17.50.
Short Handbook of Communist Ideology. Synopsis of the *Osnovy marksizma-leninizma* with complete index. 1965, XIV + 98 pp., ƒ 19.75.

—*Das Widerspruchsprinzip in der neueren sowjetischen Philosophie.* Die Moskauer Tagung zur Frage der dialektischen Widersprüche 21.-26. April 1958. Texte ausgewählt, übersetzt und eingeleitet von N. Lobkowicz. 1960, VI + 90 S., ƒ 14.35.

VRTAČIČ, L.: *Einführung in den jugoslawischen Marxismus-Leninismus.* Organisation. Bibliographie. 1963, X + 208 S., ƒ 29.50.

MONOGRAPHS

BLAKELEY, T. J.: *Soviet Scholasticism.* 1961, XIII + 176 pp., ƒ 19.75.

BLAKELEY, T. J.: *Soviet Theory of Knowledge.* 1964, VIII + 203 pp., ƒ 24.00.

LOBKOWICZ, N.: *Marxismus-Leninismus in der ČSR.* 1962, XVI + 268 S., ƒ 35.50.

JORDAN, Z. A.: *Philosophy and Ideology.* The Development of Philosophy and Ideology in Poland since the Second World War. 1963, X + 600 pp., ƒ 58.00.

MÜLLER-MARKUS, SIEGFRIED: *Einstein und die Sowjetphilosophie. Krisis einer Lehre.* Band I: Die Grundlagen. Die spezielle Relativitätstheorie. 1960, XVI + 481 S., ƒ 43.75.

PLANTY-BONJOUR, G.: *Les catégories du matérialisme dialectique.* L'ontologie soviétique contemporaine. 1965, VIII + 203 pp., ƒ 27.00.